C000120053

## Acknowledgments

We have attempted to acknowledge the authorship of both the heritage prayers and the pithy quotes that are included in this volume. Some are used with the tag 'attributed to'. Such are quotes I have found in other articles, or have over the years scribbled down in notes taken while attending lectures and seminars, or have heard quoted on radio or TV. I cannot be certain of their provenance.

It has been a delight to include a number of quotes from a recently published book combining prayers by Ron Gordon, and some superb poems of his daughter, Jennie Gordon. I thank them both for permission to place some of their fecund insights in this volume. (See *'Dad and Daughter'* www.dadanddaughter.net).

Thanks also to my long-time friends, the Rev. Dr. Norman Young, the Rev. Dr. David Beswick and the Rev. Robert Renton for their permission to borrow some of their thoughts.

A major debt of gratitude is due to my insightful proof-reader Martin Prewer, also to my honorary (and unflappable, ever-gracious, long-suffering) secretary Helen Hall, whose eye for detail and many wise suggestions have kept me out of much trouble.

Also a whopping big thank you to my USA publisher, Mary Catharine Nelson of Ideas into Books Westview Publishers, without whose most generous spirit, indefatigable enthusiasm, and publishing nous, this collection of prayers would never have been put together and made available in printed form.

Out of God's fullness I continue to be showered with unequivocal mercy heaped upon mercy.

Bruce D. Prewer
Epiphany, 2016

# Brief Prayers for Busy People

## Bruce David Prewer

Ideas into Books®
**WESTVIEW**
**Kingston Springs, Tennessee, USA**

*Ideas into Books*<sup>●</sup>
W E S T V I E W
P.O. Box 605
Kingston Springs, TN 37082
www.publishedbywestview.com

ISBN 978-1-62880-090-6

First edition, Easter 2016

Front cover photograph by Bruce D. Prewer.

Interior layout and design by Helen Hall.

Digitally printed on acid free paper.

## Dedication

To that Awesome Other who persists in using 'crude clay pots' such as I am to convey something of the glory of the grace of our Lord Jesus Christ, the love of God, and the fellowship of the Holy Spirit.

# Contents

# Introduction

Prayer takes many forms, uses varied language or silence, and addresses many needs. This book offers a compilation of over 700 shorter prayers, with the hope that some folk might be helped by some of them.

*Each day of the year has three items*: one brief, pithy quotation followed by two prayers. The first prayer is from my hand and soul, the second prayer for the day is from the rich, ecumenical heritage of humanity. I have attempted to make the latter as 'user friendly' as possible by updating archaic language where deemed appropriate.

*There is not a common theme linking each of the three items* on any given day. They are deliberately diverse in the hope that on any given day the reader might find some apposite snippet to tease the mind and feed the soul. This book can be used in communal situations, such as daily, family prayers or other group situations.

However, when compiling these pages, *I particularly had in mind those individuals who have not as yet been able to establish a regular habit of daily prayer.* During my long ministry, many good folk have confided that apart from spontaneous 'spot prayers' during a day, set times for prayer are not common. Yet they say they feel guilty about this deficiency.

My advice has always been blunt. *First, stop feeling guilty*; such guilt is a self-indulgent waste of energy. *Secondly, just start doing it!* Set aside a time each day, morning, noon or evening, and just do it. Don't give up. Stay with this daily discipline for at least twelve months.

*Maybe you are in a similar situation?* If so, this book might be of help to you. If you do not know where to start, I offer you (below) one simple method. It is a method that is more like contemplation than 'saying your prayers'.

Because of the 'moveable feasts' and seasons of the Christian calendar – *Transfiguration, Ash Wednesday, Lent, Holy Week, Good Friday, Easter and Pentecost* – I have not been able to include those themes on specific dates. However, there are some relevant prayers at times when these seasons overlap. Also, there is an appendix with prayers for those special occasions.

## One Simple Method of Daily Prayer

Each day, set aside a minimum of ten minutes to be strictly alone, with no phone, iPad or other sources of interruption. I cannot emphasise this enough. Discipline and disengagement with daily matters is essential. Get yourself into a quiet place.

Open up this book, find the appropriate date, and start reading the three items set for that day. Read slowly, savouring any phrase that speaks to your heart and soul. Stay with such meaningful phrases and absorb them, even wallow in them! And ask God to assist you to apply them to yourself and those people who are around you.

If nothing 'clicks' with you, don't persist that day. Try again next day, and the next. Lightly mark with a pencil any thoughts that do resonate with your soul; later, on those occasions when nothing 'clicks' you, you could return to a phrase you previously have found helpful. Should you miss a day, don't make a big 'guilt trip' out of it. Try again the next day.

If after a year you have not derived some blessing, then by all means hand this book to a friend and try some other method. But please, do not give up or try to ignore your spiritual hunger. Finding an appropriate way for you to commune with the Awesome Friend is well worth the effort.

It has been said that if the human mind devoted as little time and discipline to dedicated thinking as most folk do to praying, then humanity would not yet have even invented the wheelbarrow.

# Brief Prayers for Busy People

**January 1**

*For everything there is a right season, an opportune time for every activity under heaven.*

> *Qoheleth, 'The Preacher', Ecclesiastes, date unknown*

Open up our lives, loving God,
    to the opportunities of every season.
In the season of success,
    give us gratitude and humility.
In the season of frustration,
    give us patience and serenity.
In the season of failure or sin,
    give us truth and sincerity.
And in the season of repentance
    saturate us with your mercy and peace.
Amen!

*Loving God, you have chosen the weak things to confound the mighty, please send forth your continual light upon us who watch for you; that our lips may praise you and our deeds glorify you. Through Jesus Christ our Lord. Amen.*

> *Salisbury Prayers, England, c. 1100*

**January 2**

*Keep away from people who try to belittle your ambitions. Small people always do that, but the really great make you feel that you too, can become great.*

*Mark Twain, author, USA, 1835-1910*

I bless you, God my Holy Friend,
    for your ongoing gift of growing pains;
thanks for both the new challenges you set me
    and the 'perks' you lovingly deny me.
You are indeed a God of many mercies;
    be with me throughout the time to come.
For your name's sake.
Amen!

*O Lord of time and eternity, you make us creatures of time that, when time is over, we may attain your blessed eternity. With time as your gift, give us also wisdom to redeem the time, lest this day of grace be lost. For our Lord Jesus Christ's sake. Amen!*

*Christina Rossetti, poet, England, 1830-1894*

**January 3**

*If you should have only one prayer, let it be simply this: 'that your days might be a blessing to others'.*
                    *Thomas Traherne, poet-mystic, England, c. 1637-1674*

Loving God,
    look with mercy on those for whom this new year
    seems to hold more threat than promise:
refugees, orphans, prisoners and addicts,
    girls and young women sold as sex slaves,
    starving children, the unemployed or terminally ill.
Please be with them all, and help the rest of us
    to work at finding better ways and means
    of implementing that practical, costly love
which is the very spring and outflow
    of the gospel of grace, mercy and peace.
Amen!

*You, God, are the light of the minds that know you, the joy of the hearts that love you, and the strength of the wills that serve you; grant us so to know you, that we may truly love you, and so to love you, that we may fully serve you, whom to serve is perfect freedom, in Jesus Christ our Lord. Amen!*
                    *St. Augustine, Bishop of Hippo, North Africa, 354-430*

**January 4**

*What could inspire me more to cherish others than knowing that
God loves each soul as if they were the only one?*
                    *Lady Julian of Norwich, mystic and theologian, England,*
                                                        *1342-1416*

God of purest love,
    some people are so zealous
  about the affairs within your house
    that they don't notice the beggar at the gate.
Others are so distressed
    by the plight of beggars they rarely come inside
to worship with fellow disciples
    and feast at your table of love.
Please give us the balance of Jesus:
    who from the diverse fibres
of both the sacred and secular
    did weave a seamless life of love.
To your honour; Amen!

*We thank you, Father, for your holy name, which you have made
alive in our hearts, and for the knowledge, faith and immortality
which you have revealed to us through Jesus. To you be glory
throughout all ages!*
                    *The Didache, 'The Teachings', Syria, c. 120*

**January 5**

*The world is charged with the grandeur of God;*
*It will flame out, like shining from shook foil.*
*Gerard Manley Hopkins, priest and poet, England, 1844-1889*

Blessed are you, Joy of the universe,
    you give us the opportunity of a new day
and make the sun to rise and shine
    on both good and bad alike,
and send your gentle rain from heaven
    to fall on both saints and sinners.
Help us to begin this day's duties cheerfully,
    to persist with tough tasks doggedly,
to accept any failure graciously,
    to succeed humbly,
and to conclude this day thankfully.
    Amen!

*O You who are heroic love, keep alive in our hearts that*
*adventurous spirit which makes your people scorn the way of*
*safety, so that your will be done. For so only shall we be worthy of*
*those courageous souls who in every age have ventured all in*
*obedience to your call, and for whom the trumpets have sounded*
*on the other side; through Jesus Christ our Lord. Amen!*
*John Oldham, poet and scholar, England, 1653-1683*

**January 6**

*So great a sweetness flows into the breast*
*We must laugh and we must sing,*
*We are blest by everything,*
*Everything we look upon is blest.*

*W.B. Yeats, poet, Ireland, 1865-1939*

It is a very long journey, God of Magi,
    from Sydney to Bethlehem,
but in this season of joyful hopes
    we arrive with starlight in our eyes.
As we kneel, watch and wonder,
    let the radiance of your Child's face,
give us peace beyond understanding
and renewed faith to dare all in his name.
    For your name's sake.
Amen!

*Almighty and everlasting God, the radiance of faithful souls, you bring outsiders to your light, and make known to them the Son who is the true light and the bright morning star; fill, we beseech you, the world with your glory, and show yourself by your shining light among all nations; through Jesus Christ our Lord. Amen.*

*Gregorian Prayers – a compilation, Rome, c. 600*

**January 7**

*When a man surrenders all worldly ambition and rests it in God, then by mercy he has found the secret of peace.*
                    *Bhagavad Gita, Hindu Scriptures, India, c. 600 BC*

When world events seem to spin so fast
    that I am afraid of losing my foothold,
and when the rate of change tosses me about
    like bull dust in a willy-willy*,
come to me, O Spirit of quietness,
    and gather me up into the great stillness
of your unflappable love, joy and peace.
    Through Jesus Christ our Lord.
Amen!

*willy-willy = small tornado*

*Great One, creator of father sun and mother earth, we honour you for the light of moon and stars that shine at night on my country and its creatures. Let your true and sacred light in brother Jesus, make camp among our mob that we may begin to see your shape and face in both friend and enemy.*
                    *Attributed to an Indigenous Australian, date unknown*

**January 8**

*Have courage for the great sorrows in life, and patience for the small ones. And when you have laboriously accomplished your daily tasks, go to sleep in peace, for God stays awake.*

*Victor Hugo, author, France, 1802-1885*

Today, Divine Healer,
    we pray for all the sick and fearful:
The mentally unstable who each day
    struggle against fears and cruel voices;
for the victims of accidents who endure
    months of pain and tough-love therapy;
and the diseased for whom every day
    is a struggle against discomfort or distress.
Bless each sufferer at this moment,
    strengthen each to both cope and conquer.
Through Christ our Saviour;
Amen!

*Be to me, O God, a bright flame before me, a guiding star above me, a smooth path beneath me, and a kindly shepherd beside me, today, tonight, and forever. Amen.*

*St. Columba, missionary, Iona, 521-597*

**January 9**

*My overcoat is worn out; my shirts also are worn out. And I pray to be allowed to have a lamp in the evening; it is indeed wearisome sitting alone in the dark.*
> *Written from prison by John Wycliffe, Bible scholar, England, c. 1330-1384*

Though this body grow weaker,
    let us be strong in you;
though the mind become stiff,
    let us stay young in you;
though our faith be small,
    let us grow large in you;
though our love is flabby
    let it be toughened by you:
through your enduring faithfulness;
    In Christ's name;
Amen!

*God of many names, it is right that we should seek you. You alone know how to make the rough smooth, the tough tender, the misfit belong, the chaotic harmonious, and the antagonist our friend. Deliver us from the folly of wickedness, banish it, Great Father, from our souls, and relying on you may we find the wisdom to embrace your universal ways.*
> *Cleanthes, stoic philosopher, Greece, c. 300 – c. 232 BC*

**January 10**

*There are two important things about the Gospel: believe it and then do it.*
    *Susannah Wesley, scholar and educationalist, England, 1669-1742*

God of Jesus, where are your clowns?
    Where are those faithful souls in today's world
    who are content to be fools for Christ sake?
We confess too many of us have embraced conformity
    instead of your non-conformist, regenerative Spirit,
    and have traded rainbow-faith for grey respectability.
We praise you for the one or two fools in most congregations –
    those ardent souls who gamble everything on your kingdom
    and who let the chips fall where they may.
Where are your clowns today, Lord?
    Indeed, maybe they are here, beside you in our midst;
    but am I still numbered among them?

*Lord, we pray that you will open our eyes to recognise the heaven that lies about us in which we, who are born into your new life, will walk every day of this new year, and most gladly serve you with clearer vision and greater joy.*
    *R.L. Stevenson, novelist and poet, Scotland and Samoa, 1850-1894*

**January 11**

*Sentimental love may appear pretty. But Christ's costly Love as the true centre of all life and beauty, as the genius and spirit of valid religion, is something that sentimental lovers are not always eager to entertain.*

*P.T. Forsyth, theologian, England, 1848-1921*

O you who are Love Divine,
    save us from lovelessness.
The demands of importunate people
    leave us weary and irritable.
Do not allow us to become cynical,
    or to cease caring for others.
Stop us from trying to do everything,
    but also save us from shutting our door
on those – especially among the bothersome folk
    whom you send to us for help.
To the praise of your steadfast love.
Amen!

*Loving God, please be a light to my eyes, music to my ears, sweetness to my taste, and full contentment to my heart. Be my sunshine by day, my food at the table, my repose at night, my assistance in trouble. Dispose of what I am and all that I have, as you think best.*

*Bishop John Cosin, liturgist, Durham, 1594-1672*

**January 12**

*Faith is no more a burden to a man than wings are to a bird or sails are to a ship.*
                    *Samuel Rutherford, Puritan minister, Scotland, 1600-1661*

Please direct my days,
    most loving Spirit,
that I may step out this day.
    with humble confidence
to do what needs to be done;
    neither being distracted
by insidious self-doubts
    nor oblivious to the gifts
of those to whom we minister
    or who seek to minister to us.
In the name of Jesus,
    son of the carpenter
    and true Son of God.
Amen!

*I am weak, O Lord! If I ever ask for favours from you, please don't listen to me. And even if you do hear, please don't act upon it. Let your will alone be fulfilled. My only happiness lies in what pleases you. I don't even know what is good for me! Whatever you do is the best, even if I don't understand it.*
                    *Jalalaldin Rumi, poet-mystic, Afghanistan, 1207-1273*

**January 13**

*Whoever sets any bounds for the reconstructive power of the religious life over the social relations and institutions of men, to that extent denies the faith of the Master.*
*Walter Rauschenbusch, Baptist social activist, USA, 1861-1918*

Lord Jesus, Friend of Sinners,
    so you want us to love everyone,
even our enemies and tormenters?
    Now that does leave me gob-smacked!

You know, Lord, I'll need a triple transfusion of grace
    to counter my inclination to strike back.
If I am to become one of your peacemakers
    it will only happen by your empowering Spirit.
Amen!

*Author of all things seen and unseen, we hold out our empty hands to you: we pray for your mercy, your pity, your continuing benevolence; correct our faults and increase in us strength, faith and understanding. Send to us angelic spirits to guide us in your ways of genuine holiness. Amen.*
*Serapion, Bishop of Thmuis, Egypt, c. 350*

**January 14**

*blessedness basks*
*at the dark and dangerous edges*
*of this life*
*and suffocates*
*in the secure and safe centre.*
                    *Jennie Gordon, UCA minister and poet, Australia, born 1962*


Loving God,
    pour your healing Spirit today and always:
on the sick and those who nurse them,
    on workers and all who employ them,
on the unemployed and those who support them,
    on the hungry and all who feed them,
on refugees and those who welcome them,
    on drug addicts and all who treat them,
and on the sorrowing and those who comfort them,
    Through Christ Jesus our Servant Lord.
Amen!


*Please, loving Father, give faith to beginners, intelligence to the*
*little folk, aid to those who run the race, sorrow to the careless, a*
*passionate spirit to the tepid, and to all the faithful, a good ending.*
                    *St. Irenaeus, Bishop of Lyons, France, c. 200*

**January 15**

*All who call on God in true faith, praying earnestly from the heart, will certainly be heard, and will receive what they have asked and desired.*

*Martin Luther, protestant reformer, Germany, 1483-1546*

When I fear I am alone on a misty sea,
    with no one to hear my cry or notice me,
there comes the creak of rigging and sail,
    then through the gloom I glimpse a small craft
with one lone Sailor at its helm
    whose hand never wearies.
Blessed are you, Master Mariner, Jesus Christ,
    my joy and my salvation!
Amen!

*O Abyss, O eternal God, O sea profound, what more could you give me than yourself? Clothe me, clothe me with yourself, eternal truth, that I may run this mortal race with true obedience, and always live in the light of your most holy faith.*

*St. Catherine of Siena, Dominican mystic, Italy, 1347-1380*

**January 16**

*The Son calls us to venture beyond the safeguards of the law to the risky business of love.*
> *Ron Gordon, UCA minister and writer, Australia, born 1932*

Loving God, we are glad
    there are no hospital visiting hours
    able to restrict your presence.
Wherever there are patients in distress,
    let your Spirit come
and spread a mantle of tranquility
    over all your suffering children,
    whether they believe in you or not.
Through Jesus, your best physician,
    we offer this prayer.
Amen!

*God, make each moment of our lives a miracle.*
    *God make us laugh at the impossible.*
*God give us hope when all seems hopeless,*
    *peace where no peace could be,*
    *and love for the unlovable.*
*Make us gamble on all your Almightiness,*
    *and to dare everything in your great service.*
> *Adelaide E. Procter, poet, England, 1825-1864*

**January 17**

*Show love to every creature and you will be happy and whole; for when you love all things, you are a loving God, who first loves them each and all.*

*Tulsidas, poet and reformer, India, c. 1532-1623*


I thank you, God, for untamed things:
    desert wombats and sea eagles,
    mountain trout and wild donkeys,
    welcome swallows and great whales;
and the best of all we say thanks
    for the untameable, resurgent,
    ever-living Son of Man,
    the giver of intrepid faith and liberty.
Wonderful are you, Friend of the earth
    and Joy of loving hearts!
    Be praised, amazing God, forever!
    Amen!


*Holy Spirit, you have chosen to make us your playmates; please lead the child within each of us in your wonderful ways. Fuse us into one team, you in us and we in you, until we could not be closer, and remain so unwearied forever.*

*Mechthild of Magdeburg, mystic and social activist, Germany, c. 1207 – c. 1282*

**January 18**

*Earth's crammed with heaven and even common bush afire with God; but only he who sees takes off his shoes.*
*Elizabeth Browning, poet, England, 1806-1861*

In your Presence, Joy of the universe,
    we celebrate that we are creatures
who are made for, and sustained by, your light:
    dawn-light over city towers
    candle-light on lovers' faces
    noon-light bouncing on ocean waves
    red ochre-light in outback places.
Much more we celebrate Christ your True Light:
    Bethlehem, Nazareth and Galilee light
    hidden Gethsemane and Cross light
    and unquenchable Easter light.
Most beautiful, everlasting and joy-full Light.
    Heaven and earth are full of your glory!
    Amen!

*Come Spirit of Truth, evermore enlighten us and dismiss all cloud and dross.*
*Christina Rossetti, poet, England, 1830-1894*

**January 19**

*Look inwards, for you have a lasting fountain of happiness within you that will always bubble up if you will but dig for it.*
*Marcus Aurelius, Emperor, Rome, 121-180*

God of all seasons,
    on this cloudy, asphalt-grey morning,
when even song birds sit desultory on dead tree limbs,
    tune my heart to the Infra-Melody
    which underpins all things.
As from a deep and sparkling artisan lake,
    release in me a gusher of delight,
and, like desert wildflowers after rain,
    festoon my spirit with praise.
    Amen!

*Lord Jesus, have you forgotten we exist? Many of us are waiting for you to come and help: the war-scarred are waiting for peace, the hungry are waiting for a bite to eat, the refugees are waiting for a homeland, the sick are waiting for healers. O Lord, come quickly, we pray.*
*A prayer from Uganda, 20th century*

**January 20**

*Pure faith penetrates to the furthest deeps of heaven and even now takes possession of joys yet to be.*
*Hippolytus, reformer and Bishop, Rome, c. 170 – c. 236*

Good morning, most wonderful Friend!
  Good morning Joy of loving hearts!
    Good morning, Spirit that fills all things!
    God of each new day and year:
Please give us a 'make over' by your Spirit,
  and let loving praise begin to reshape
  all my thoughts, words and actions.
    Through Jesus Christ our Lord.
Amen!

*O God we thank you for this earth, our home; for the wide sky and blessed sun, for the sea and streams, for the everlasting hills and the never-resting winds, and for trees and the common grass underfoot. We thank you for our senses by which we hear the song of birds, see the summer fields, taste the autumn fruits, rejoice in the falling of snow, and smell the breath of spring. Save our souls from being so blind that we pass unseeing when even the common thornbush is aflame with your glory!*
*Abbreviated from Walter Rauschenbusch, Baptist social activist,*
*USA, 1861-1918*

**January 21**

*During prayer I become one in spirit with God, and through him I actually become united by faith and love, with those people for whom I am praying.*

*John of Kronstadt, priest and mystic, Russia, 1829-1908*

Loving God, we come
not because we are good,
    but because your name is love;
not because we have the answers to life,
    but because you are abundant life.

Be with us in this congregation,
    brush us with the breath
    of your ever gentle
    but eternally strong Spirit.

Recreate within us
    all that expresses clearly
    your authentic love and life.
    For Christ's sake,
    Amen!

*Living or dying, Lord, I would be yours; keep me as your own child for ever, and draw me day by day nearer to yourself, until I become wholly filled with your love, and fitted to see you, face to face.*

*E.B. Pusey, theologian and scholar, England, 1800-1882*

**January 22**

*I can explain none of it! The mystery of God's being and action can only be pointed to, and then only with pictures and metaphors.*
        Norman Young, minister and theologian, Australia, born 1930

God of Jesus and our God,
    you are elemental Wisdom.
When many sophisticated atheists
    cannot see beyond their noses,
you give to the poor and the meek –
    those who are fools for Christ's sake –
a vision of your exponential future
    which is an awesome wisdom
    and an indomitable delight.
Wherever there are minds willing to perceive,
    hearts to receive and souls to believe,
blessed are you, Joy of the Universe,
    Amen!

*Grace-giver, holy Friend, give us the sense to want you, the eagerness to seek you, the patience to wait for you, the insight to recognise you, the passion to meditate on you, and deeds that praise you. Through the dynamic of the Spirit of Jesus Christ, our Lord. Amen.*
        St. Benedict of Nursia, monk, Italy, 480 – c. 547

**January 23**

*Yes! You should set a definite time each day for deliberate prayer.
Do this and the spirit of prayer should more and more penetrate all
your wakening hours.*
> Baron von Hügel, spiritual director, Austria and England,
> 1852-1925


Saviour-Friend,
    many of us have become slaves to virtual reality:
    electronic illusions now stifle imagination,
    harden hearts and tutor us to be artificial.
Come to our aid, Spirit of grace and truth,
    redeem us from bondage to illusions,
    save us from everything that is less that real
    and deliver us into the authenticity of your Spirit.
Amen!


*God be in my head and in my understanding;
God be in my eyes and in my looking;
God be in my mouth and in my speaking;
God be in my heart and in my thinking;
God be at my end and at my departing.*
> Salisbury Prayers, England, c. 1100

**January 24**

*When deeds outstrip learning, learning prospers, but when learning exceeds one's good deeds, learning becomes a useless corpse.*

*An old Hebrew saying*

We pray, God of all people,
    for a future where all get a fair go;
where the lucky guys
    will not lord it over the unfortunate,
nor the stronger ones
    force their will on the weaker.
Let your justice flow around us
    like abundant waters,
and your righteousness
    like an ever-flowing stream.
      Let this be, dear Lord,
    let this be.
Amen!

*Many a chilled heart, O my God, has been set aglow with the fire of your Presence, and many a slumberer has been wakened by the sweetness of your voice. Many are the weary wanderers who have sought cool shelter in the shade of the oasis of your goodness, and numerous the thirsty ones who have panted after for the springs of your living waters.*

*Adapted from Bahá'í Prayers, originally from Persia, 19th century*

**January 25**

*It is an enormous headache to be a Christian in Australia today, but God makes it bearable.*
                    *Fifteen-year-old boy, Australia, date unknown*


Blessed are you, Heart and Hope of the universe;
        you have given us this ancient continent
        to be our temporal home and school,
and have called us to become worthy stewards
        of the land and its creatures and its beauty,
        of its people, its hopes and its destiny.
Please become the Activist in our ranks
        and the scourge of sloth and apathy,
that we may do much better than before
        and not rest self-satisfied
until we hear your approval:
        "Well done come, share the joy of your Lord."
Amen!


*Grant, Lord, that we may hold to you without parting, worship you without wearying, serve you without failing; faithfully seek you, happily find you, and forever possess you, the only God, blessed now and forever.*
            *St. Anselm, Archbishop of Canterbury, England, 1033-1109*

**January 26  Australia Day**

*The Great South Land of the Holy Spirit*
> *Pedro de Quiros, explorer, Portugal, 1565-1614*
*The most godless place under heaven*
> *James Denney, theologian, Scotland, 1856-1917*

God of aborigine and boat people,
>  of both old and new Australians,
grant us the ability to celebrate this Day.
>  without cant or triviality.
Where repentance is needed
>  help us to repent with integrity.
Where honour is warranted,
>  let us wear it with humility.
Where new goals are overdue,
>  make them your goals, not ours.
Through Jesus Christ our only Master.
>  Amen!

*Lord, bless our land and its citizens, that faith and love may season the hearts and minds of all our leaders and all those who follow their lead. Fill them with a new love for your ways, that with a fresh vision of justice and mercy they may become the true trustees of the gifts you have granted them.*
> *Adapted from William Laud, Archbishop of Canterbury,*
> *1573-1645*

**January 27**

*A queer country, Australia, so old that, as you walk on and on, there's a feeling comes over you that you are gone back to Genesis.*
*Attributed to an Australian pioneer, date unknown*

We praise you,
  Holy friend, for those solitary places
in tall forests or by the ocean,
  on outback mountains or by rivers,
where we are enabled to simply let go
  of our disabling tensions or worries,
and, led by your Counsellor-Spirit,
  we may just relax and quietly belong
to the beauty and rugged energy
  of your creative handiwork.
Amen!

*Lord, teach me how to seek you, and reveal yourself to me when I do. For I cannot seek you, unless you teach me, nor ever find you unless you reveal yourself. Let me search for you in my longing and long for you in all my searching. Let me find you in my loving and love you in my finding. I know you have created me for this, to be aware of you and truly love you.*
*St. Anselm, Archbishop of Canterbury, England, 1033-1109*

**January 28**

*What good does our arrogance finally do for us? The arrogant are like ships that pass by on the waters; in a short time there is no trace that they have ever been.*

*Book of Wisdom, Alexandria, Egypt, c. 100-40 BC*

Lord of history, source and destiny of Days,
please give us a vision of the future
 devoid of the puerile propaganda of 'progress'.
Give us persistent and resilient faith
 in the ongoing redeeming work of Christ Jesus.
Remind us each morning of your ability
 to bring good out of evil and new growth from decay.
Let us know and fully trust the Spirit
 who neither faints nor grows weary.
Through Christ Jesus our Redeemer.
 Amen!

*You, living God, are the light of the minds that know you, the joy of the hearts that love you, and the strength of the wills that serve you; grant us so to know you, that we may truly love you, and so to love you, that we may fully serve you, whom to serve is perfect freedom; in Jesus Christ our Lord.*

*St. Augustine, Bishop of Hippo, North Africa, 354-430*

**January 29**

*At the hour of prayer the very stars, trees and rivers pause for a moment, and the entire universe celebrates and praises God together.*
> *Hippolytus, reformer and Bishop, Rome, c. 170 – c. 236*

Loving God, in your majestic stillness
    where I know for sure nothing can contain you
    no words define you, no prayer manipulate you,
there alone do I find most available
    my deepest security, my holiest serenity
    and the purest praise and adoration.
Hallelujah!

*Lord, I thank you that in my old age you have taken away all earthly wealth, and that you now clothe and feed me through the kindness of others. Lord, I thank you that since you have taken away the sight of my eyes, you serve me now through the eyes of others. Lord I thank you that since you have taken away the strength of my hands and my heart, you minister to me by the hands and hearts of others. Lord, most dearly I pray for them; reward them for it in your heavenly love, that they may faithfully serve and please you until they too reach a happy end.*
> *Mechthild of Magdeburg, mystic and social activist, Germany,*
> *c. 1207 – c. 1282*

**January 30**

*Laugh and the world laughs with you, whinge and you whinge alone.*
*Adapted from Ella Wheeler Wilcox, poet, USA, 1850-1919*

Good morning, lovely God!
   Nearby doves cooing,
   overhead planes soaring,
   city traffic rumbling;
today I offer to your glory
   everything my eyes perceive,
   every skill my hands display,
   every sound my ears receive
every prayer that I might pray,
   every path my feet explore
   every impulse to adore.
   Through Christ Jesus our Master,
Amen!

*O Searcher of hearts, you know us better than we know ourselves.*
*You see the sins that our very sinfulness hides from our own eyes.*
*Lift us up from where we have fallen, and keep us from sin today.*
*Fill us with a holy simplicity, content to seek and do your will.*
*James Martineau, Unitarian scholar, France, 1805-1900*

**January 31**

*There are times in worship when the soul must launch out in triumphant affirmation against all that is senseless and dark in the world. Then, to say 'I believe' becomes the noblest act of which a human being is capable.*

*Précis of a quote from L.P. Jacks, Unitarian minister and philosopher, England, 1860-1955*

You, our hidden yet most loving God
    who are the giver of faith,
enable us to doubt our own doubts
    with the same stringency
as that which we commonly bring
    to the credulity of others.
Take what little faith we do have
    and in the laboratory of your Spirit
put it through your unique process
    of purification and condensation,
until it is clear and humble enough
    for you to put it into active service.
Amen!

*Look, before you is an empty mug that needs to be filled, Lord, please fill it. I am cold in love; warm me and make me fervent, that my love may reach out to my neighbour. I do not have a strong and stable faith; at times I doubt and am unable to trust you completely. O Lord, help me. Strengthen my faith and trust in you. Amen!*

*Martin Luther, protestant reformer, Germany, 1483-1546*

**February 1**

*Every child who is born in this world arrives with the message that
God does not despair of humanity.*
                          *Rabindranath Tagore, poet, India, 1861-1941*

Lord Jesus Christ,
you call us to this very day
    from diffidence to confidence,
    from deficiency to adequacy,
    from dithering to doing.
Bathe us in your buoyant Spirit
    and energise us with your strong
    and exuberant selflessness.
For your love's sake.
    Amen!

*Most holy Friend, please continue your mercy to us and bless us,
and let your smiling face beam upon us. Help us to make known
your loving ways in all the world, and spread your liberation and
healing among all nations.*
                                  *From Psalm 67, Old Testament*

**February 2**

*Jesus evidently felt deeply the emptiness and futility of much religious talk. He was interested only in those emotions and professions which could get themselves translated into character and action.*
*Walter Rauschenbusch, Baptist social activist, USA, 1861-1918*

Wonderful God, you are
our gracious and joyous Paradox:
    please close my ears that I might hear,
cloud my mind that I might know,
    clip my thoughts that they might soar,
still my tongue that I might sing,
    and take my life that I might live abundantly.
For your love's sake.
    Amen!

*Loving God, in you alone we find our full humanity. You give us the will to hope when there seems nothing left to hope for, and the power to love others even when we feel unlovely. May it be so for us, this day. Amen!*
*Based on writings of Jürgen Moltmann, theologian, Germany,*
*born 1926*

**February 3**

*But above all other things, Spirit, I love thee –*
*Thou art love and life! O come,*
*Make once more my heart your home.*
                    *Percy Bysshe Shelley, poet, England, 1792-1822*

Loving God,
     as we prepare to go to bed,
renew not only tired bodies
     but also the hidden depths
of our complex psyche where
     hope and compassion,
faith, wisdom and love,
     are made and nurtured.
Let us rise tomorrow,
     rejuvenated and eager.
To your praise and glory!
Amen!

*God, my Father and Friend, I praise you for all you have given me,*
*and for all you have taken away from me; Be with me, Lord for the*
*time to come. I do not know what is before me, but you know.*
*Choose my portion for me; lead me by your own hand, and keep me*
*close to you, day by day and night by night.*
                    *Ashton Oxendon, Bishop of Montreal, Canada, 1808-1892*

**February 4**


*Is prayer your steering wheel or spare tyre?*
*Attributed to Corrie ten Boom, Christian social activist,*
*Netherlands, 1892-1983*


Blessed are you, Joy of the universe!
  O generous Creator of time and space,
loving Saviour of fools and rebels,
  joyful Counsellor of the children of light,
yours is the kingdom of hope-fullness,
  the power of saving grace,
and the awe-full grandeur
  of the crucified and risen Christ,
forever and ever.
Amen!


*As you were with me at my life's first shaping*
  *please be so again at my journey's end.*
*Be with me each day at my rising and working,*
  *please be with me in sleeping, surrounded by saints.*
*Be with me each hour in my seeing and hearing,*
  *please be with me at the end and bring me safely home.*
*As you were with me before my beginning*
  *please be so again far beyond my ending.*
                              *Traditional Celtic prayer*

**February 5**

*I have looked around a lot, and done a lot of thinking, and have concluded that both evil and greed are forms of insanity.*
*Attributed to Qoheleth, 'The Preacher', Ecclesiastes,*
*date unknown*

God most wonderful, while I thank you for the mercy that covers all our sins,
I also give thanks for the grace that has saved me from committing even more:
   for the revenge not taken and forgiveness not withheld;
   for the gossip not passed on and condemnations not uttered:
   for injustices not ignored and compassion not withdrawn;
   for the lies not told and the sexual temptation not yielded to;
   for the faith not compromised and my Lord not denied;
   For the times when the Word has been validated
   in the rough and tumble of my own daily busyness,
   as "grace is made perfect in human weakness",
all thanks and praise be to you, my Saviour and my God.
   Amen!

*Most merciful Redeemer, Friend and Brother, may we know you more clearly, love you more dearly, follow you more nearly, day by day. Amen and Amen!*
*Richard, Bishop of Chichester, England, 1197-1253*

**February 6**


*Some things you learn best in a calm, and some in a storm.*
                    *Attributed to Willa Cather, novelist, USA, 1873-1947*


Holy Friend, my Redeemer, with
    all the costliness of your saving grace,
    all the ruggedness of your ways,
    all the serenity of your strength,
    all the disruptivity of your love,
    all the simplicity of your wisdom,
unfold your healing enormity within me.
    For your name's sake.
Amen!


*Bless, my little garden plot and the joy with which I'm tilling it,*
*Bless the hopes I'm planting and prayers with which I'm filling it.*
*Bless the seasons that are coming and the sunshine and the rain.*
*Bless my home and my health and the health of my wee bairn.*
*Bless, O Father of good giving.*
*Bless, O Son of redeeming.*
*Bless, O Spirit of the living.*
*Bless, O Holy Three all-loving.*
                    *Adapted from a traditional Celtic prayer*

**February 7**

*A soul that is dominated by fastidiousness, is as yet only hovering round the precincts of Christianity, but it has not entered its sanctuary.*

> *Baron von Hügel, spiritual director, Austria and England,*
> *1852-1925*

God, you are not choosey;
    you love ugly characters
and find signs of hope
    where we become cynical.
Give us more of your attitude
    in our inclinations and actions.
Let our commitment to loving
    be less selective more generous,
For we too are the sinners
    for whom Christ died.
Through Christ Jesus, our Lord.
    Amen!

*Use me, my Saviour, for whatever purpose and way you require. Take my heart for your abode, take my mouth to spread abroad your glory, take my love for the health of believers. May I never allow the steadfastness and confidence of my faith to abate.*

> *Dwight Moody, evangelist, USA, 1837-1899*

**February 8**


*You are only giving a trifle when you give of your money; it is when you give yourself that you truly give.*

*Kahlil Gibran, poet, Lebanon, 1883-1931*


On this glistening morning,
    we pray, loving God, for those
    whose eyes seem so clouded
that they cannot see the light:
    the insolvent farmer, the deserted mother,
    the rejected social misfit, the neglected child,
    the prisoner sighing, the drug addict crying.
Please bless all those kind hands
    that will reach out to them
    with practical loving.
Amen!


*Speak with me, Lord, for your servant is listening. Speak words of encouragement into my willing ears. Please speak to me in words and I shall try to speak with my deeds. For Christ's sake, Amen.*

*Alexander Pope, poet, England, 1688-1744*

**February 9**

*The realm of God is like a housewife who, wanting to make some bread, took some yeast and 'hid it' in an enormous amount of flour (about 130 cups!) until the whole dough was leavened.*

*Joshua, the son of the 'Baker Woman'*

God of bakers and homemakers,
    and the bread of common life,
please knead us with your grace,
    and season us with your beauty,
so that no duty may seem beneath us,
    no person too crude to befriend,
and that no calling from you
    may seem beyond our ability
as long as you remain with us
    with the fecund energy of new life.
Amen!

*Grant, O Lord, that we welcome all truth, under whatever forms it may be a uttered, and have the goodwill to receive new thoughts with graciousness. May we bless every good deed, no matter who does it, and rise above party strife and slogans to the contemplation of your eternal goodness.*

*Charles Kingsley, minister and social reformer, England, 1819-1875*

**February 10**


*The lowest ebb is at the turning of the tide.*
*Henry Wadsworth Longfellow, poet, USA, 1807-1882*


When we seem battling through spiritual fog
    and landmarks are shrouded,
please pilot us, insightful Lord,
    in our going out and our coming in.
May those who travel with us
    travel more safely because your hand
    is resting firmly on ours.
Thank you for never forgetting us
    or forsaking us.
Amen!


*Creator God, we thank you for the mass of stars with which you
have spangled the raiment of darkness, giving beauty to the world
when the sun withdraws. Yet all this magnificence is but a little
sparklet that has fallen from your Presence; for you are the Central
Fire of all things and the Radiant Light among all, and the heavens
are but dim reflections of your wisdom, your power, and your glory!*
*Theodore Parker, minister, USA, 1810-1860*

**February 11**

*We can live without religion and meditation, but we cannot survive
without human compassion.*
> *Attributed to the 14th Dalai Lama, Tibet and India, born 1935*

God most loving,
help us to nurture neighbours,
    not as a substitute for you
    but as a sharing in your outreach
    and a caring for your beloved.
Let us not be put off
    by any superficial dislikes
    nor patronise the meek and poor
    with attitude, word, or deed.
In all we attempt to do alongside others
    give us the graciousness of Jesus
    the guidance of your Holy Spirit
    and the resources of your Fatherly love.
    Amen!

*Lord Jesus, save us from over-zealous self-examination, from
straining and scraping the bottom of our soul. Let us quietly wait for
you to show us what needs to change; and may we then have the
faith to follow, be it painful or easy. For your love's sake.*
> *Based on a letter of Evelyn Underhill, author and mystic, England,
> 1875-1941*

**February 12**

*His (Christ's) otherness comes to us both as a judgment on our limited humanity and as the ground of our hope for the fulfilment of our humanity as the children of God.*
*David Beswick, UCA minister and psychologist, Australia,*
*born 1933*

God of immense galaxies and quantum peculiarities,
    while astronomers at Siding Springs and Mt Wilson
    probe more of the mind-blowing stuff of outer space,
save us from writing ourselves off as trivial specks
    inhabiting one unimportant little planet.
Remind us that it is we who are the astronomers,
    and it is you alone who have given us the curiosity
to seek, find, explore and delight in
    your trans-cosmic surprises and glory!
Amen!

*God there is no other like you, among all the stars or on earth, keeping faith with people and inviting us to keep faith with you. No temple or shrine can hold you, no mind or heart enfold you; heaven itself cannot contain you, nor the angels comprehend you. Yet in your heavenly dwelling place you will always hear our prayers.*
*Attributed to King Solomon, Jerusalem, c. 950 BC*

**February 13**

*Prayer is the world in tune, a spirit voice and vocal joys whose echo is heaven's bliss.*

*Henry Vaughan, poet, England, 1622-1695*

Holy Friend, you are the hope
    of everything that draws breath,
    the life of creatures great and small.
Without your Spirit
    the koala cannot climb,
    the cockatoo cannot call,
    the young wallaby cannot caper.
Without your breath
    we homo sapiens can't exist,
    neither can we hear Christ's call
    nor create a community of love.
We love you, we worship you,
    Source and Soul of loving hearts.
Through Jesus our brother, your Holy Son.
Amen!

*Pour upon us, O God, the spirit of love and family-kindness, so that refreshed by the dew of your blessing we may delight in your glory and grace. Through Christ our Lord.*

*Salisbury Prayers, England, c. 1100*

**February 14**

*Our human predicament stems not from the fault of some lower nature, but from the perversity of our best self, the image of God.*
    *Norman Young, minister and theologian, Australia, born 1930*

Jesus, brother of James and Jesse,
continue to embrace us;
    what is wounded, heal;
    what is wrong, discipline;
    what is over-sensitive, toughen;
    what is rigid, bend;
and what is cold and barren,
    prepare for that spring season
    which we know you will send
    in your good time.
For your love's sake.
Amen!

*O my dear God, help me to walk in the way of love which does not look first for self in anything. Let me love you for yourself, and love nothing else but in and for you. To give all for love is a most sweet bargain. Let me love you only as you want me to love you*
*For your name's sake. Amen.*
        *Gertrude More, Benedictine nun, England, 1606-1633*

**February 15**

*A master in the art of living draws no sharp distinction between his work and his play; his labour and his leisure; his mind and his body; his education and his recreation. He hardly knows which is which.*
*L.P. Jacks, Unitarian minister and philosopher, England,*
*1860-1955*

O Delight of the morning star,
O Delight of mellow dusk,
   of my childhood and youth
   of my maturing and ageing;
fill me to overflowing
   with your zest for life.
Fill my home and family,
   my friends and neighbours
   and all my workmates;
yes, fill even my enemies
   with the new wine
   of abundant life.
Wonderful are you, my Lord,
   the Delight of loving hearts!
Amen!

*Lord, you share your light with your friends that they may be your reflectors, bringing your light to bear on human affairs – achievements and failures, victory, defeat, suffering, life and death. May your people add light to the lives that have become confusion, and add hope where folk have lapsed into hopelessness.*
*Adapted from Ron Gordon, UCA minister and writer, Australia,*
*born 1932*

**February 16**


*Sleep that knits up the ravelled sleave of care*
*The death of each day's life, sore labour's bath,*
*Balm of hurt minds, great nature's second course,*
*Chief nourisher in life's feast.*
          *From 'Macbeth', William Shakespeare, poet and playwright,*
                    *England, 1564-1616*



Lord, have mercy
     on your overtired children
     who are finding it hard
     to get a good night's sleep.
Overcome their fears,
     relieve their guilts,
     release their tensions,
and close their eyelids
     with the fingertips
     of your gentle caress.
Amen!



*Christ Jesus, you are the bridle of wild horses, the wings of the sea*
*eagle, the rudder of ships, and the shepherd of the Kings lambs.*
*Gather together your children who love you with simplicity; let*
*them rest in your goodness, and rise up at dawn to sing of your*
*holiness and celebrate with sincerity your guiding hand and your*
*loving ways.*
          *Clement of Alexandria, theologian, c. 150 – c. 215*

**February 17**

*I don't mind the thought of suddenly dying because my bags have been already packed.*

*Attributed to Pope John XXIII, 1881-1963*


The deepest peace of the loving Creator be yours:
    the peace of the flowing rivers and the wooded hills,
the peace of the snow-capped mountains and frosted plains,
    the peace of summer evenings and playing children,
the peace of the midnight stars and the Southern Cross,
    the deep, deep peace of eternal Love be always yours.

The deepest peace of the loving Redeemer be yours:
    the peace of Bethlehem and the shepherds' fields,
the peace of prodigal sons and good Samaritans,
    the peace of healed lepers and forgiven enemies,
the paradoxical peace of the cruel cross and the empty tomb,
the deep, deep peace of the eternal Saviour be always yours.
    Amen!


*You, Holy Friend , are my light and salvation, of whom then need I fear? You are the very strength of my living, of what then need I be afraid?*

*Psalm 27:1, Old Testament*

**February 18**


*Now the man has a child*
*he has also learned the names*
*of all the local dogs.*

*Senryū Karai, poet, Japan, 18th century*


O Holy One,
in the grey-light of immanent dawn,
I heard you saying unto me:
> Come unto me all you who are overworked
> and who carry heavy burdens
> and I will give you sweet relief.
Awesome Friend, I hear what you say;
please make me a doer of your word;
to your eternal honour;
> Amen!


*Teach us, O gracious Lord, to begin our daily tasks with eagerness,*
*to go on with obedience, and to finish them in love; through Jesus*
*Christ our Lord.*

*George Hicks, Bishop, England, 1642-1715*

**February 19**

*Everybody, my friend, everybody lives for something better to come.*
*That's why we want to be respectful of every man; who knows*
*what's in him, why he was born and what he can do?*
                                    *Maxim Gorky, novelist, Russia, 1868-1936*

Loving God,
    never for one moment permit us
    to treat any person or creature as unimportant,
    to be exploited or abused at will,
but to respect all things as consecrated
    by your creative Providence,
    by your mothering Spirit,
    and by the enabling grace of Christ Jesus.
Amen!

*Loving God, pardon our past ingratitude and disobedience, and*
*purify us from all contamination, whether by your gentle or more*
*drastic dealings, till we have finished your work on earth and you*
*remove us to your own Presence with the host of the redeemed in*
*heaven. Amen!*
                                    *Mary Carpenter, social reformer, England, 1807-1887*

**February 20**

*Do what you feel in your heart to be right, for you'll be criticized anyway. You'll be damned if you do and damned if you don't.*
        *Attributed to Eleanor Roosevelt, politician, USA, 1884-1962*

Lord Jesus, help us to walk bravely with you.
Please bring your gift of light not only to our outward sight
    but also to our inner vision.
Make us children of light and ambassadors of your love,
    that we may walk bravely where in the past we have faltered.
If we look like chickening out, please steady us,
    should we crash, then please pick us up once more.
May we achieve more than we have a right to,
    and live with a courage that is not of our own making.
Amen!

*The peace of God, our only peace, the peace of Mary, loving and kind, the peace of Christ, king of tenderness: rest upon each window, upon each door, upon each space that lets light in, upon the four corners of my house; upon each thing my eye takes in, upon each thing my mouth takes in, upon my body made from dust. The peace of Christ, king of tenderness: rest on my body made of dust, rest on my spirit from on high.*
        *Adapted from a traditional Celtic prayer*

**February 21**

*You will never enjoy the world properly until you wake up each morning and find yourself in already in heaven; see yourself in your Father's palace, and look upon the skies, the earth and the air as celestial joys.*

Thomas Traherne, poet-mystic, England, c. 1637-1674

Holy Spirit, Soul of Love,
    unleash your abundance within me
until every faculty is transfused
    with your healing ministry;
that I may gain the vision
    to discern the footprints of Christ
in this twenty-first century
    and follow wherever he leads me.
To the praise of the Name that is timeless
    and the glory of the Love that is boundless.
Amen!

*God, look generously at your whole church, that wonderful and sacred mystery, and carry out the work of our salvation. Let the whole world feel and see that things which were cast down are being raised us and things which had grown old are being made young, and all things are returning to perfection. Through Jesus Christ our Lord. Amen!*

Gelasian Prayers, France, c. 6th-7th century

**February 22**

*My dear sisters and brothers, this is a time for seeking; for seeking and finding; a time for earnestness; if you find yourself touched, it will most deeply touch home.*
                    *Jacob Boehme, shoemaker and mystic, Germany, 1575-1624*


God of dusk and the evening star,
      as we seek our rest in you,
renew not only tired bodies
      but also our hidden depths
where hope, faith and love,
      are made and nurtured.
Let us rise from fatigue
      rejuvenated and eager.
Amen!


*Please give us, Father-God, a clean start for beginners, intelligence to the young, aid to those who are doing it tough, repentance to those who fall, a revived spirit to those who are lukewarm, and to those who have given their best, a good ending.*
                    *St. Irenaeus, Bishop of Lyons, France, c. 200*

**February 23**

*We can never know things at their worst till we stand where they
are at their best. The worst is our sin; and we will never resile to it
until we have made the best of it in God.*

P.T. Forsyth, theologian, England, 1848-1921

Lift from our shoulders,
    most blessed Redeemer,
    every burden of guilt,
and save us from the tyranny
    of mulled-over regrets.
Renew our dented faith,
    and purify our love.
Wherever we can, let us undo wrongs
    without making a big display of it;
By the strength of your Spirit
    and to the praise of your Name.
Amen!

*Lord God, you have given your people the dignity of the forgiveness
of sins through the washing of the Holy Spirit; by your saving grace
within them may they serve you always. For yours is the glory,
Father, Son and Holy Spirit, in the holy church now and for ever and
ever. Amen!*

Hippolytus, reformer and Bishop, Rome, c. 170 – c. 236

**February 24**

*Sin is a social force. It runs from man to man along the lines of social contact. Its impact on the individual becomes most overwhelming when sin is most completely socialised.*
    *Walter Rauschenbusch, Baptist social activist, USA, 1861-1918*

God, we are the idiots* whose riches have become our poverty:
    we crowd our homes with things but are short on love;
    we focus on electronic images yet rarely look into human eyes;
    we stagger under a load of information but are light on nous;
    we have plenty of advisors but not enough practitioners;
    we rush around as tourists yet rarely live as pilgrims.
Saviour Christ,
    have mercy your crazy sisters and brothers,
    confront us with our spiritual penury
    and make us eager for the gifts of the Spirit.
Amen!

*some scholars claim the Greek word 'idiotes' was, in primitive Greek, used for a miser who clutched his possessions to himself.*

*God, of your goodness, give me yourself; for you are sufficient for me. I cannot properly ask anything less, to be worthy of you. If I were to ask less, I would always be in want. In you alone do I have all. Amen!*
                    *Lady Julian of Norwich, mystic and theologian, England,*
                                                              *1342-1416*

**February 25**

*Cleave the wood and you will find me, lift up the stone and I'll be there.*

*Attributed to Christ Jesus, Gospel of Thomas, c. 140*

Have pity, loving God, on us your perverse creatures,
    who work technological miracles yet little real progress;
we can restore sight, move mountains, fly through space,
    yet we have not learned how to share our daily bread,
we make deserts blossom and implant new heart-valves
    yet seem unable to live together in peace,
we can heal the sick, banish demons, and sometimes even
    wake the dead, yet find it difficult love one another.
Please, rescue us from the enigma of our own being;
    give us the desire and the will to be saved.
Help us to grasp more of that wholesome goodness and delight
    prepared for those who employ your gift of faith.
For your love's sake.
Amen!

*O my God, let me walk in the way of that love which does not know how to be selfish. Let me love you just for yourself, and nothing else but in you and for you. Let me love nothing instead of you; to give all for love is a most sweet bargain.*

*Gertrude More, Benedictine nun, England, 1606-1633*

**February 26**

*In so far as we love compassion and practice it steadfastly to that extent we resemble our heavenly Creator.*
Mechthild of Magdeburg, mystic and social activist, Germany,
c. 1207 – c. 1282

Holy God, awesome Friend of sinners,
    please interfere in my life as you see fit.
Make me hungry for whatever your deem valuable,
    and to strive for it with undivided tenacity.
Help me to show uncalculated love to whomsoever you wish,
    and to cherish those pleasures which most delight you.
With every gram of my free will I beg you:
    "Please don't allow me to screw up!"
Within your redeeming grace, let this be, dear Lord.
Amen!

*Deep peace of the running wave be yours.*
*Deep peace of the flowing air be yours.*
*Deep peace of the quiet earth be yours.*
*Deep peace of the shining stars be yours.*
*The deep, deep peace of the Son of peace be yours.*
*From a Celtic benediction*

**February 27**

*live your life bright,*
*fully flavoured*
*in the sway of God*
              Jennie Gordon, UCA minister and poet, Australia, born 1962

O loving Christ, from pernicious religion
    deliver your easily mislead people:
Save us from trusting our fickle feelings
    and deliver us into faith in your saving grace;
Save us from complacent placidity
    and deliver us into the realm of your disruptive peace;
Save us from facile good intentions
    and deliver us into the realm of your proactive love;
Save us from clutching at easy answers
    and deliver us into the realm of your Mystery;
Save us from petty little ambitions
    and deliver us into the realm of your holy cross;
For your name's sake.
    Amen!

*O Lord, may I never lose, as years pass away and the heart shuts up*
*and all things seem a burden, let me never lose this youthful, eager,*
*love of you. Make your grace supply the failure of my nature. Do the*
*more for me the less I can do for myself.*
          John Henry Newman, Cardinal, England and Ireland, 1801-1890

**February 28**

*It was not long before the Enemy suggested; "This cannot be faith;*
*where today is your joy."*
> John Wesley, clergyman and evangelist, England, 1703-1791
> *(just one day after his conversion at a fellowship meeting at*
> *Aldersgate Street, May 24, 1738)*

Holy Friend, please deliver me
    from my own crowded, hyper-thoughts.
Cut through this internal cacophony
    and bring me to your quiet place
    of green pastures and still waters.
Let me stay there with you, you alone,
    until my disordered mind is redeemed
    by the beauty of your gospel of peace.
Through Christ, your sure shalom.
    Amen!

*O God the Father, Origin of Divinity, the good that is beyond all*
*good, lovely beyond all that is lovely, in you there is calmness,*
*peace and harmony. End the arguments that divide us from each*
*other, and bring us back to a unity of love, which will bear some*
*likeness to your divine nature. Through the grace, the mercy, and*
*the tenderness of your Son, Jesus Christ. Amen!*
> *Dionysius Telmaharensis, Patriarch, Syrian Orthodox, 818-845*

**February 29   (Leap Year)**


*One should never consent to creep when one feels the impulse to soar.*
*Helen Keller, deaf-blind social activist, USA, 1880-1968*


God of light, love and awesome joy,
since we have been keeping company with your Son,
    a new passionate music is swelling within and among us;
    we yearn for an end to the old human order
    with its broken shards of melody and paranoid discords.
We long to move freely across old borders,
to be citizens of a new international realm
    where each one is free to become a little Christ,
    where broken melodies are mended and complete,
and the neglected harmonies of our humanity
are restored to a beauty and rapture
    like nothing the ear has ever heard before
    nor the mind conceived.
For your love's sake.
    Amen!


*I take my rest in bed,*
*as a child in its mother's arms.*
*Whether I awake here or hence*
*I lie safe in your generous keeping,*
*You victorious Child of Mary.*

                      *Traditional Celtic evening prayer*

**March 1**

*The greatest honour we can give Almighty God is to live joyfully because of the knowledge of his love.*
> *Lady Julian of Norwich, mystic and theologian, England,*
> *1342-1416*

Most awesome Friend,
   you are the light of the dreary and the life of the weary.
Like the merry old sun cascading into chill valleys
   and bathing desert peaks with glory,
cascade your love upon us this day and saturate us
   with the irrepressible grace of our Lord Jesus Christ,
   the unfathomable, steadfast love of God,
   and the intimate companionship of the Holy Spirit.
Then our dreariness shall give away to delightfulness
   and our weariness become usurped by liveliness;
   for your name's glory.
Amen!

*O beloved Saviour, show yourself to those who knock, that knowing you we may love only you, desire only you, think only of you and fill our minds with you by day and night. Awaken within us the fullness of love that is worthy of your glory.*
> *St. Columbanus, Irish missionary, France, 543-615*

**March 2**

*Don't search for God in the wilderness, for God is already in your heart.*
*Sikh Scriptures, the Granth, c. 1469-1708*

Spirit of liberty and of costly love,
please dwell with all your suffering people
whose outward liberties are few:
    some are forbidden to worship,
    some are denied professional advancement
    some are languishing in prison,
    and some are called to die for your name's sake.
Holy friend be with them through every crisis,
    and may the peace of Christ garrison their hearts,
    the courage of the Spirit fortify their spirits,
    and the salvation of God rescue their bodies
    from all distress, injustice and abuse.
Amen!

*Heavenly Friend, the Encourager, the Spirit of Truth, you are present*
*in all places, filling all things; you are the treasury of goodness, the*
*choirmaster of life. Come and make your home within us, clean out*
*all dust and grime and wash our souls until they shine.*
*St. John Chrysostom, Archbishop of Constantinople, Rome,*
*c. 347-407*

**March 3**

*What, I ask, did Christ see in you but yourself? He is the true lover who longs for you, not for anything that is yours.*
           *Peter Abelard, scholar and theologian, France, 1079-1142*

Great Creator and Redeemer,
     you alone are the Holy One!
You are the light beyond the light of a billion suns;
     you are the hope beneath the hope of a billion prayers;
you are the love within a billion loving actions;
     and you are the prodigal grace of our Lord Jesus Christ.
Mighty Friend,
     holy is your name, holy are all your deeds of redemption.
Amen!

*Lord, stop us from being self-centred in our prayers and teach us to pray for all outsiders. May we be so bound up in love with those for whom we pray, that we may feel their needs as keenly as our own, and to seek their blessing with sensitivity, empathy, and imagination. We ask this in Christ's name. Amen.*
           *John Calvin, Protestant reformer, Geneva, 1509-1564*

**March 4**

*Salvation is a social force. It is exerted by groups that are charged with divine will and love. A full salvation demands a Christian social order which will serve as the spiritual environment of the individual.*
*Walter Rauschenbusch, Baptist social activist, USA, 1861-1918*

God, our refuge and strength,
    when in the ongoing struggle
for justice mercy and peace
    excessive weariness besets us
almost overwhelming us,
    help us to just hold on.
Then, should doubts begin to mock
    our only partly successful results,
help us to hold on yet again.
    Through the blessing of your Son
and in the fellowship of your Spirit.
Amen!

*Brother Jesus, Saviour and Master, I know that all have sinned as I have sinned, and each has added to the Enemy's net of evil. Yet one better thing I also know: the magnitude of human stumbling can never extend beyond the measure of God's mercy. This makes me adventurous for you, and it gives me wings! You are the most wonderful, the most beautiful, my Brother, my Saviour my Master!*
*Symeon, the New Theologian, Constantinople, 949-1022*

**March 5**

*Have courage for the great sorrows in life, and patience for the small ones. And when you have laboriously accomplished your daily tasks, go to sleep in peace; God is always awake.*

Victor Hugo, author, France, 1802-1885

Emmanuel, you do not hand out favours
    to shield believers from disasters,
but you share our ordeals
    and suffer in our sufferings.
Grant to all who are at this moment
    in agony of body or mind,
an acute awareness of your Spirit,
    so that even in deepest distress
they may be granted fellowship with you.
    In Christ's loving name.
Amen!

*Loving Lord, assist me to be content with the present moment, and less anxious about the future, and with an accepting mind submit to any loss I do have, or to any disappointment in my expectations. Amen.*

Simon Patrick, Bishop of Ely, England, 1626-1707

**March 6**

*who lies unnoticed and unattended*
*on the other side*
*of your locked door*
*covered with the wet breath of dogs*
   *if you were only willing*
   *to see them?*
      *Jennie Gordon, UCA minister and poet, Australia, born 1962*


Abba-God, bless our family
   with the gift of a generous spirit,
that the love we share together
   in the security of home
may liberate us
   to love our neighbours
   and to pray for our enemies.
Through the Spirit of Jesus,
   our brother and Lord.
Amen!


*Lord of Light, may faithfulness defeat disorder in this house; may peace triumph over conflict, generosity over selfishness, respect over contempt, true speaking over lying words; and may right living conquer the demon of deceit here in this house.*
      *The 'Jasna', Zoroastrian, c. 6th century BC*

**March 7**

*Love all of God's creation, of the whole and every grain of sand within it. Love the animals, love the plants, love everything. When you love the smallest things you will begin to see the divine Mystery everywhere.*
*Fydor Dostoevsky, author, Russia, 1821-1881*

God our Creator and Redeemer,
the Holy Providence:
    field-lily and wild raven, wombat and bilby,
    tree-fern and platypus, rainbow and billabong,
    seed and gestation, pensioner and nation.
Indefatigable Providence:
    parental caring and sharing, in our laughing or weeping
    fearing or daring, never weary nor sleeping,
    joyful as the sunrise, hopeful as children's eyes.
We thank and praise you,
    God our Creator and Redeemer.
    Amen!

*Lord, what a precious gift you have given me! In every person that you have made you have given a resemblance of yourself for me to enjoy! Could any ambition of mine have aspired to such treasures?*
*Thomas Traherne, poet-mystic, England, c. 1637-1674*

**March 8**

*A Christian is the most free Lord of all, and subject to none.*
*A Christian is the most dutiful servant of all and subject to everyone.*
*Martin Luther, protestant reformer, Germany, 1483-1546*

God of Christ Jesus, please continue to probe
    and renew us with the Gospel stories.
There is something of the prodigal son in us
    who needs to come to his senses;
there is within us something of the street woman
    who needs to weep at your feet;
there is something of the leper in us
    who needs the touch of a loving hand;
and there is something of the lost-yet-found sheep
    that needs to hear the angels singing for joy.
God of parables, please continue your gospel story within us,
    convert our hearts and carry us through each day's duties
with a grateful and cheerful spirit.
    Through Christ Jesus our delight and salvation.
Amen!

*Lord Jesus, may the sweet yet fiery passion of your love absorb my*
*soul completely, and make it a stranger to anything that is not of*
*you or for you. For your Name's sake.*
*St. Francis of Assisi, friar, Italy, 1181-1226*

**March 9**

*By the alchemy of grace, no sin of mine can ultimately frustrate the purposes of God.*
> *Lady Julian of Norwich, mystic and theologian, England,*
> *1342-1416*

Shaper and keeper of the Southern skies,
    at night the sign of the Cross
    rises and sets over our land.
Grant that the hour may come
    when the Man of the Cross
    will rise up into every heart,
    every street, office, and parliament.
May the love of Christ flourish,
    and joyful lives celebrate.
Amen!

*Lord, bless our country, that faith and love may season the hearts and minds of all our leaders; those who stand out among us, all politicians, judges, scholars, the rich, powerful and influential. Fill them with a new love for Your ways, that with justice and mercy they may become the very salt of the earth and worthy trustees of the gifts you have loaned to them. Through Jesus Christ our Lord.*
> *Adapted from William Laud, Archbishop of Canterbury,*
> *1573-1645*

**March 10**

*In the Cross of Christ I glory, towering o'er the wrecks of time.*
*John Bowering, politician and diplomat, England, 1792-1872*

Messiah Jesus, Lamb of God,
    God of Golgotha,
how much you suffered for us,
    we only dimly comprehend.
All our best phrases and theories
    seem trite in the presence
of your majestic, humble loving
    which chooses to reconcile all things.
Yet we know, Lamb of God,
that you take away the sin of the world,
    and you grant, even us, your peace.
Holy, holy, holy, crucified Redeemer,
    all things are filled with your glory!
Amen!

*Lord of light, please listen to our prayers, and forgive both our conscious and unconscious transgressions. For with you there is plenteous redemption, and we commend our spirits to your mercy, with thanks and praise. Amen.*
                                                    *Eastern Orthodox prayer*

**March 11**


*(On rampant capitalism) God for us all and everyman for himself, said the elephant as he danced among the chickens.*
                                              *Charles Gore, Bishop, England, 1853-1932*


Save our nation, merciful God,
      from the blandishments of mammon,
      where daily the ranks of the rich swell
      while the multitude of the poor grows.
The spawn of this injustice
      includes despair, muggings and shootings,
      so that no longer do people walk
      the streets easily by night.
Save us, Lord, or we all shall perish;
      sting us with your Spirit,
      restore in us neglected values
      and recall us to the unseen riches.
Let us trust Christ and his spiritual athleticism
      and follow only him.
Amen!


*Lord, it seems you have taken away all the blessings that I once had from you. In your grace, please give me now that one gift which every dog seems to have by nature – that of being faithful to you in my distress, faithful even when all comfort is gone. This I desire more fervently than a seat in your heavenly kingdom.*
      *Mechthild of Magdeburg, mystic and social activist, Germany,*
                                                    *c. 1207 – c. 1282*

**March 12**

*The cleverest one of all, in my opinion, is the man who calls himself a fool at least once a month.*
                    *Fydor Dostoevsky, author, Russia, 1821-1881*


Holy friend, we know our human predicament;
    that evil contaminates everything –
    even the good things we try to achieve;
but what exacerbates our human predicament
    is our grave ignorance and sordid stupidity
    which frustrates the efforts of even the wisest.
So we beg you, Saviour of the world,
    not only to forgive our many sins
but also to override our ignorance to mend
    the rents we make in the fabric of community.
Into your wise, humble and loving hands
    we commend all that we are and want to achieve.
Amen!


*God the Father of our Lord Jesus Christ, please multiply in us faith, truth and gentleness, and grant us a place and a task among your saints.*
                    *Polycarp, Bishop of Smyrna , c. 69 – c. 155*

**March 13**


*Love is all we have, the only way that each can help the other.*
                    *Euripides, dramatist, Greece, c. 480 – c. 406 BC*


Today, Lord, I watched
    a neatly-dressed man,
    with downcast eyes,
    go from bin to bin
    salvaging cans and bottles.
He looked up once, noticed me,
    then moved quickly past the next bin,
    pretending he was putting something in.
O Lord, what has my nation become
    that the unemployed now eke out a living
    by doing what kids used to do
    for pocket-money?
Lord have mercy.
    Christ have mercy.
    Lord have mercy.
Amen!


*God, grant me*
*the serenity to accept the things I cannot change,*
*the courage to change the things I can,*
*and the wisdom to know the difference.*
                    *Reinhold Niebuhr, theologian, USA, 1892-1971*

**March 14**


*Great God, if Christ is truly your revealer,*
*the living image of the hidden Lord,*
*then you also must be a wounded healer*
*pierced to the heart by wanton deed and word.*
> *Inspired by G.A. Studdert Kennedy, poet and priest, England,*
> *1883-1929*



Loving Creator and blessed Redeemer,
always in the crowds around us are
    the unhearing ears, the songless tongues,
    the aimless feet, the empty hands,
    the joyless eyes and the lost souls.
Yet you did not intend
    that it should remain so.
By the example and word of Christ,
    maintain the rage of our compassion
    until all have ready access to the justice
    and love which the gospel proclaims.
For your love's sake,
    Amen!



*O God, give me victory over myself, that nothing may imprison my*
*soul. Be the guiding light of my spirit, lift me up from the dark*
*troughs. May my soul, enraptured by your wisdom, fight its way*
*upwards in fiery flight. For you alone understand me, and only you*
*can give me the inspiration to keep on going.*
> *Attributed to Beethoven, composer and pianist, Vienna,*
> *1770-1827*

**March 15**

*He is richest who is content with the least, for contentment is the
true wealth of nature.*
                    *Socrates, Athenian philosopher, Greece, 469-399 BC*

Most Holy Friend
    let us die to greed that we may live generously,
let us die to grudges, that we may live mercifully,
    let us die to pride that we may live humbly,
let us die to guilt that we may live freely,
    let us die to apathy that we may live lovingly.
let us die to anxiety, that we may live boldly:
    Through Christ Jesus, our blessed redeemer.
Amen!

*Lord, you have been patient, infinitely patient with me. Yet I have
been impatient for measurable results, ready to give up and forsake
you. As I receive your merciful peace, grant me the conviction that
nothing can rob me of it; neither my foolish earthly desires, nor my
wilder longings, nor the hungry anxieties of my heart.*
                    *Adapted from Soren Kierkegaard, philosopher, Denmark,*
                    *1813-1855*

**March 16**

*The godless may see themselves as very reasonable people, but a chip on their shoulder will make them blind as moles.*
                    *Attributed to King Solomon, Jerusalem, c. 950 BC*

Christ Jesus, you are the blessed laser of God;
    pierce the clouds of our ignorance,
    correct the distortion in our vision,
    lance the abscess of our self-interest,
    cut away the scar tissue of old hurts
    and cauterise the weeping sores of our fears.
We trust ourselves into your unshakeable hands
    for whatever radical treatment you choose.
Through Christ Jesus, our light and our healing.
    Amen!

*Glorious God, do not allow me to trade my soul for earthly prizes. I trust the small boat of my soul to you, for you alone can pilot me home through currents and rapids. When I approach the straits of death, open your eyes wider and enlarge your care of me, so that no weakness or darkness may shake my trust or blind my soul. For Christ's sake. Amen.*
                    *Adapted from John Donne, poet and preacher, England,*
                    *1572-1631*

**March 17**

*I pray that you cling*
*to the Love that upholds you*
*when life is dismantled*
*and nothing remains.*
                *Jennie Gordon, UCA minister and poet, Australia, born 1962*

Only your saving grace can free us,
    only your grace can inspire us,
    only your grace can resource us;
only you can give us the energy
    to become, in spirit and deed,
    what we were created to become.
Bless us, Lord Jesus, with your liberty
    that we may experience the rapture
    of being the children of God.
Amen!

*I lie down in my bed*
    *as someday I will lie in the grave,*
*with your arm pillowing my head*
    *and your hand holding my soul.*
*Love shall be at my head,*
    *love shall be at my feet,*
*love shall be my new hope*
*and love shall be my peace,*
    *you victorious Child of Mary.*
                        *Traditional Celtic evening prayer*

**March 18**

*For it is not in death that men die most.*
                    *Elizabeth Browning, poet, England, 1806-1861*

O blessed Redeemer,
    do not cease from your rugged companionship,
    lest we falter and look back over our shoulder.
By the fiery love of your indwelling Spirit
    make us bolder than we have been
    and more loving than we thought likely.
O most resourceful Redeemer!
    O faithful Friend of sinners!
O Rapture of the friends of God!
    Hallelujah!

*Deliver your people, God,*
    *from politics without principles,*
*from wealth without work,*
    *from pleasure without conscience,*
*from knowledge without character,*
    *from commerce without ethics,*
*from worship without sacrifice,*
    *and from science without a soul.*
            *Attributed to Mahatma Gandhi, India, 1868-1948*

**March 19**

*What to others seems like day time, is night to the spiritual man who truly sees.*

*Bhagavad Gita, Hindu Scriptures, India, c. 600 BC*

We praise and thank you, Giver of grace:
    for the clean doubts that bless us,
    for the hard questions that unsettle us,
    for the deep mysteries which baffle us,
and for those awe-full moments
which leave us wide-eyed with awe.

We praise and thank you, Giver of grace:
    for the truth that arrests us,
    for the light that strip-searches us,
    for the self-awareness that humbles us,
and for those awe-full moments
which leave us aching with awe.
Amen!

*Make us worthy, Lord, to serve our fellows throughout the world who live and die in poverty and hunger. Give them, through our hands, this day their daily bread. And by our understanding love, give joy and peace. Amen!*

*Attributed to Mother Teresa, religious sister and missionary, Calcutta, 1910-1997*

**March 20**

*I will cling to Christ Jesus like a burr clings to a coat.*
   *Katie Luther, wife and soul-mate of Martin, Germany, 1449-1552*

If we have preferred pious rituals rather than the pursuit
of justice and mercy;
   bring us to repentance.
If we have tried to be socially respectable rather than
being fools for Christ's sake,
   bring us to repentance.
If we proliferate excuses rather than pick up our cross
and follow Jesus unconditionally,
   bring us to repentance.
Lamb of God, you take away the sin the world,
have mercy on us and grant us your peace.
   Amen!

*Teach us, good Lord,*
*to serve you as you deserve,*
*to give and not to count the cost,*
*to fight and not to heed the wounds,*
*to toil and not to seek for rest,*
*to labour and not to ask for any reward*
*save that of knowing we do your will.*
   *St. Ignatius Loyola, founder of the Jesuit Order, Spain, 1491-1556*

**March 21**

*A ruffled mind makes a restless pillow.*
*Charlotte Bronte, writer, England, 1816-1855*

Teach us, Holy Friend, how to stay calm
    even when we are at the heart of a storm.
Rescue us from those divided loyalties
    which foster frustration and angst,
heal us from that exaggerated self-importance
    which adds to our worries,
and deliver us from an unrepentant stubbornness
    which locks us into an uptight life-style.
Return us to that radical, undivided soul and mind
    which is the core peace of Christ Jesus.
Amen!

*Grant us, O Lord, the grace not to set our hearts on material things,*
*but to love things more spiritual. Even while we must spend our*
*days among things that have no permanence, assist us to cleave*
*heartily to those qualities that abide forever. Amen.*
*Pope Leo the Great, Rome, c. 400-461*

**March 22**

*All men were made by the same Great Spirit Chief. We are all brothers. The Earth is the mother of all people, and all people should have equal rights upon it.*

*Heinmot Tooyalaket, Native American, USA, 1840-1904*

This morning the world is aglow
with the glory of creation,
    yet the crows and the wagtails
    are squabbling again!
God, I ponder a fallen world;
    all the human violence,
    broken bodies and broken minds.
I long, I yearn painfully,
    for that new world
Where even crow and wagtail
    shall live together in peace
and nations learn war no more!
    Please God!
Amen!

*Good God, please say for me an 'amen' to my prayers, if what I request be your gracious will; but if in anything I have asked or done amiss, pardon my infirmities, and answer my necessities, for Jesus and his mercies' sake. Amen*

*Thomas Wilson, Bishop, Isle of Man, 1663-1755*

**March 23**

*The real objectivity of the Atonement is that sacrifice is not made to God but by God.*

*P.T. Forsyth, theologian, England, 1848-1921*

Loving God, maybe this is the day
    when some of us slack Christians
will wake us up to ourselves
    and become shocked by what we see.
Please deliver each of us
    from unrepentant remorse
and turn our faces towards
    the crucified Friend of sinners.
Generate in all of us a hunger
    for Christ's word and way,
and raise up within us the gift of salvation
    that we may dare to step up to really live it!
Amen!

*All I try to do, Lord, will fail without your aid; Only your Spirit can save me; let it flow through mind and feelings redeeming all that is corrupt yet hidden behind the weak the walls of my body.*

*Michelangelo, painter-sculptor, Italy, 1475-1564*

**March 24**

*The person who is a blessing to others will be happy; those who scorn others shall know only discontent.*
                    *Attributed to King Solomon, Jerusalem, c. 950 BC*

If by our own wilfulness we have led other souls astray,
    Lord have mercy.
If in spite of good intentions we have mislead neighbours,
    Christ have mercy.
If we have been too proud to admit our faithlessness,
    Lord have Mercy.
By your grace, restore to us the joy of living grace-fully
    and renew a right spirit within us.
Amen!

*I confess to you, O God, that although I do notice other people I do not love them enough. Please supply my deficiency. Make me so to love all that I may be a blessing to all and please you in all, that we may be knit together in godly love and united in your service. To your honour and glory.*
                    *Thomas Traherne, poet-mystic, England, c. 1637-1674*

**March 25**

*Whoever is near me is near the fire.*
*Attributed to Christ Jesus, Gospel of Thomas, c. 140*

God, my beloved Enemy,
    thank you for never giving up on me;
Thank you for opposing my vanities
    and exposing my sins,
for hauling me out of every funk hole
    where I try to hide and evade
    the tough loving of the Gospel.
You are the most faithful, blessed enemy
    anyone could ever have.
May I dearly love you and heed your word
    today and for evermore.
Amen!

*O my God, I lay dozing on the couch of lonely selfhood when you woke me up with the divine accents of your voice. You unveiled your beauty to me, enabled me to hear your words, to recognize it was really you, to become grounded in your love, and enabled me to sing your praises and extol your goodness.*
*Adapted from Bahá'í Prayers, originally from Persia, 19th century*

**March 26**

*It is only hope which is really real; what is lightly called reality is but
a bitterness and a deceit.*
>    William Makepeace Thackeray, novelist, England, 1811-1863

Loving Spirit, encircle my house that it may withstand
    those who love darkness rather than light.
Encircle my loved ones, that as they sleep
    that they may be recreated by your Spirit.
Encircle my absent friends that they may be sheltered
    under the warmth of angel wings.
Encircle my enemies that during the night
    their dreams may explore your peace.
Holy Friend, encircle each of your children
    with the strong grace of Jesus, the warm love of God,
    and the sweet communion of the Holy Spirit.
Amen!

*The wisdom of all living things be yours,
wisdom of the owl and the dolphin,
wisdom of the ant and the honeybee:
    the abiding wisdom of the loving Creator
    be always yours.*
>    Adapted from a traditional Celtic prayer

**March 27**


*Be who God meant you to be and you will set the world on fire.*
          *St. Catherine of Siena, Dominican mystic, Italy, 1347-1380*


All-loving God,
    there are some days of little faith
when a primitive fear of death
    stalks me from the dark corners;
or even worse when fear of a slow, painful dying
    scares me and shakes the foundations.
Interlace the strong chords of your love
    throughout my whole being
that whatever the future holds
    I may remain faithful in spirit and truth,
truly yours, now and forever
Amen!


*Holy Spirit, please penetrate those murky corners where we hide*
*shabby memories and unsavoury inclinations. Bring into your light*
*the buried grudge, smouldering enmity, cankering bitterness, those*
*secret fears which sap our energy, and the pessimism which is an*
*insult to your joy. Loving Lord, we yield these dark things up to your*
*light, that you may cleanse and transmute them into a deeper*
*understanding of others and a larger love for you.*
          *Evelyn Underhill, author and mystic, England, 1875-1941*

## March 28

*Some contemporary Christians are in a panic; like the young jackaroo\*, who, when the herd began to stampede, jumped up on his horse and tried to ride off in every direction at once.*
*Josh Doulos, pastor, Australia, born 1965*

*\*jackaroo = apprentice cowboy*

God of long range goals and immediate tasks,
    set me free from worry and petulance.
Liberate me not only from jumping at shadows
    but also from worrying about matters beyond my reach.
So ground me in your providence
    and sweeten me with your graciousness
that I may cheerfully tackle whatever I can
    and calmly leave the rest to others.
Amen!

*Lord Jesus, open wide the window of our spirits and fill us with light; open wide the lockers of our hearts and fill us with love, open wide the doors of our minds that we may receive you and entertain you with all our power of adoration and love.*
*Christina Rossetti, poet, England, 1830-1894*

**March 29**

*When the light in a silver lamp goes out, the beauty of the lamp can no longer be seen.*
> Mechthild of Magdeburg, mystic and social activist, Germany,
> c. 1207 – c. 1282

Loving God, please do not allow us to ignore the poor and the meek,
> and may the greedy and the arrogant not get away with it forever;
have mercy on the affluent for claiming their status as a right,
> and on intellectuals for speaking big words which exclude many.
Send the liberating spirit of Jesus in to our hearts and minds
> and give our lips the simplicity of his speech,
that we may build new communities of respect, unity and love,
> wherever the Gospel is treasured and lived.
Amen!

*O Father, help us to know that the hiding of your face is wise love. Your love is not over-fond, doting and reasonless. Your bairns must often have the frosty, cold side of the hill, and must set down their bare feet among the thorns. Your love has eyes and watches over us, for our pride needs some winter.*
> Adapted from George MacDonald, preacher-poet, Scotland,
> 1824-1905

**March 30**

*he is always walking towards*
*a future*
*that breaks into our every breath*
*whispering the summons*
    *if you long to go forwards*
    *then repent, turn around.*
        *Jennie Gordon, UCA minister and poet, Australia, born 1962*

God of the bruised and wounded,
    help us to take defeats productively
    and not waste years licking old wounds.
If the defeats are merely to our own pride
    help us to recognise them as such.
Whenever the cause is your mission,
    give us the courage to take stock,
and to get ready to renew the contest,
    on another day and other front
    of your wise choosing for us.
In the name of Christ,
    Amen!

*Lord hear, Lord forgive. Lord please hear what I speak not, forgive*
*what is amiss, complete what I leave undone. Let it be that your will*
*may be done not according to my poor wants but according to your*
*mercy and truth, and may everything issue to your glory and for the*
*good of your kingdom. Amen.*
    *Maria Hare, author, England, 1798-1870*

## March 31

*When faith and hope fail, as they do sometimes, we must try charity, which is love in action. We must speculate no more on our duty, but simply do it. When we have done it, however blindly, perhaps heaven will show us why.*

*Dinah Maria Mulock, novelist, England, 1826-1887*

All-loving God,
    your true Son reckoned the cost
of the world's liberation
    in the Garden of Gethsemane,
Bring us to our knees
    and keep us from sleeping,
that we may share his distress
    and watch with him awhile.
For your love's sake.
    Amen!

*I bless you, my Friend, for all that you have given me and all that you have taken from me. You are indeed a God of love; be with me, Lord, for the time to come. Keep me close to you, day by day, night by night, and take away everything that hinders me from being altogether yours. Amen!*

*Ashton Oxendon, Bishop of Montreal, Canada, 1808-1892*

**April 1**

*From the first day to the very last night there has never been, nor
ever will be, so magnificent an action as the Cross.*
                                *Dante Alighieri, poet, Italy, 1265-1321*

God of Jesus, through the foolishness of the cross
    you are saving those who throw in their lot with your Son.
On this April Fools' Day, may we keep a sense of humour
    should others try to make idiots of us;
yet maintain within us the robust willingness
    to appear as clowns for the sake our Lord Jesus
whenever we are called to witness to his unique ways
    among the meek and the merciful, the pure and the poor.
Amen!

*God our Creator, I do not strive to understand you or the world you
have made. I cannot comprehend the reason for pain and suffering.
I just want to relieve the pain and suffering of others. I pray that as I
do it, I may understand more clearly your nature: that you are the
father of all people, and that the hairs of our heads are still
numbered.*
                                *St. Francis of Assisi, friar, Italy, 1181-1226*

**April 2**

*He who defines his conduct by legalism, imprisons his songbird in a cage.*

*Kahlil Gibran, poet, Lebanon, 1883-1931*

O Galilean sower,
    come with your gentle feet
    and perceptive eyes.
Please, softly enter
    the field of my soul
and sow your potent seed
    of disruptive, new life.
Amen!

*Eternal God, You have filled the world and adorned it with plants for perfume, healing and food, animals tamed and wild and birds that sing merrily. You have given a rhythm of years and days, changing seasons, and the scudding clouds that drop rain that fill up fruits and gives food to all. What is more wonderful, by your grace-gift we have emerged from nothingness to exercise reason and judgment, faith and love, within this paradise of delights. To you our thanks and to you our hymns, to you all praise and glory!*

*Adapted from Apostolic Constitutions, Syria, c. 375-380*

**April 3**

*Learn this lesson: If you are to do the work of God's prophet, you need is not to wield a sceptre but a labourer's hoe.*
*Bernard of Clairvaux, monk and mystic, 1090-1153*

Loving God, I would like to be able to pray with the saints,
    "Breathe into me holy and heavenly desires."
Yet I have learned that much of so-called 'holiness'
    can be as cloying as saccharine.
I have come to understand how much ego
    can contaminate good intentions and outcomes.
Therefore, awesome Friend, please do your 'holy thing'
    Deep within my being without me knowing.
Let me become a person of rigorous love,
    more like your incomparable Jesus,
    yet be completely unaware of it.
Through Christ my Saviour And Master.
    Amen!

*My Lord and my God, take me from all that keeps me from you. My Lord and my God, grant me all that leads me to You. My Lord and my God, take me from myself and give me completely to you.*
*Nicholas of Flüe, hermit and mystic, Switzerland, 1417-1487*

**April 4**

*The belief in a supernatural source of evil (the Devil) is not an absolute necessity; men alone are quite capable of every wickedness.*

*Joseph Conrad, Polish-English author, England, 1857-1924*

If we have acted like owners in a world into which we brought nothing,
    we repent, loving Creator.
If we have lived like paupers in the presence of the wealth of Christ,
    we repent, loving Saviour.
If we have existed like loners when you are nearer than the air we breathe,
    we repent, loving Spirit.
Have mercy upon us, O God, according to your loving kindness,
    and make us again the free citizens of your brave new world.
For your truth's sake.
    Amen!

*Have mercy, O God, on all who wish to harm me. Please take their faults and mine together, and in your own tender and merciful ways let your wisdom prevail in us, so that we both amend our ways and redress our wrongdoings. Bring us as saved souls together in heaven where we may ever live and love together with you and all your blessed saints; O Glorious Trinity, through the redeeming passion of our sweet Saviour, Christ. Amen.*

*Thomas More, scholar and statesman, England, 1478-1535*

**April 5**

*Why are people who live in the grace of God so keen on serving him? Because once tasting and enjoying God the soul can't stomach anything else.*

> *Meister Eckhart, author and mystic, Germany, 1260-1328*

We praise and thank you, Giver of grace:
    for the faith that upholds holds us,
    for the hope that uplifts us,
    for the love that enthrals us,
    and for those wonder-moments
    which leave us praising with awe.

We praise and thank you, Giver of grace:
    for the Arms that enfold us,
    for the Shoulders that carry us,
    in the Voice that laughs with us,
    and for those wonder-moments
    which leave us serving with awe.

*I do not know, O God, what may happen to me today. I only know that nothing will happen but what has been foreseen by you from all eternity, and that is sufficient. O my God, keep me in your peace. I adore Your eternal designs. Through Jesus Christ our Lord.*

> *Elisabeth of France, sister of Louis XVI, 1764-1794*
> *(written while awaiting execution in Paris)*

**April 6**

*There seems to be a spiritual law whereby nothing can be wholly won
or enjoyed without something being given up or sacrificed for it.*
                              *Otto Rank, psychoanalyst, Austria, 1884-1939*

To the things we should learn,
        return us, loving Lord.
From the things we should forget,
        release us, loving Lord.
Of things of which we are better ignorant,
        relieve us, loving Lord.
From those things we now repent,
        retrieve us loving Lord.
By your spirit and in truth,
        restore us, living, loving Lord.
Amen!

*God, show me the way ahead. Others seem so sure of their
Christian role. For me it's murky, not at all clear. Gosh, Lord! I'd like
to be as wise as Solomon, as patient as Job, as loving as Mary, and
as practical as Martha. But, oh God, it's just plain old me, trying
hard – sometimes too hard – trying, trying to be the kind of person
you would have me be.*
                              *June Grey, parish administrator, Australia, 20th century*

**April 7**

*So long as mists envelop you, stay and be still; be still until the sunlight pours through and dispels the mists – as it surely will. Then act with courage.*
  *Attributed to Chief White Eagle, Native American, USA, 1840-1914*

Divine Friend, by your enabling friendship
    lift from our shoulders
the burden of cares and worries
    which we have gathered on our journey.
Set them aside from us,
    and free us from after-tension.
Massage our weary being
    with the strength of your renovating love.
Let the fingers of your grace
    probe and heal those areas which are bruised.
Blessed are you, Lord of quietness;
    you bring rest to the weary!
Amen!

*When the night is starless and dark, or when the low clouds brood and colours are dimmed, there is a Light that comes: the gloom fears and shrinks, and clouds are pierced by the spear-light of Christ. From his shining face bright colours return to all things.*
  *Aurelius Prudentius, poet, Spain, 348-405*

**April 8**

*When you pray, your spirit rises to meet in the ether those who are also praying at that same moment.*
                              *Kahlil Gibran, poet, Lebanon, 1883-1931*


Yours is the goodness
    eclipsing all virtue on earth or in heaven,
Yours is the lasting beauty
    transcending all loveliness,
Yours is the generosity
    exceeding all prodigality,
Yours is the redeeming grace
    surpassing all other mercies.
Holy, holy, holy, God of countless hosts,
    heaven and earth are full of your glory!
Amen!


*Keep watch, dear Lord, with those who wake, or watch, or weep tonight, and give your angels charge over those who sleep. O Lord Christ: tend your sick ones, rest your weary ones, bless your dying ones, soothe you suffering ones, shield your joyful ones; all for your love's sake.*
        *St. Augustine, Bishop of Hippo, North Africa, 354-430*

**April 9**

*O God, when you give your servants a task to do, let us know that it is not the beginning but the continuing on with that task, until it is thoroughly finished, which will yield true glory to you. Amen.*
*Sir Francis Drake, courtier and sea captain, c. 1545-1596*

Thanks, Lord Jesus, for including me in your taskforce
  and for the enabling gifts of your Holy Spirit.
I pray for the will and skill to better do those errands
  which I have done moderately well in days past,
and to undertake new assignments, not as a leaden duty
  but as a joy that is set before me.
If I grow careless, encourage me in diligence,
  should I grow tough, restore me in tenderness.
Let me always be open to the new things
  you may wish to achieve in and through me;
through Messiah Jesus, who makes all things new.
  Amen!

*O my Lord Jesus, may everything close to your heart be my chief concern also. Let me have some surety that I am giving myself entirely to whatever you ask of me, and wherever my duty to you takes me. For your love's sake.*
*Bernard of Clairvaux, monk and mystic, 1090-1153*

**April 10**


*Oh the comfort, the inexpressible comfort of feeling safe with a person, having neither to weigh thoughts nor measure words, but pouring them all right out, just as they are.*
*Dinah Maria Mulock, novelist, England, 1826-1887*


Holy Friend, we confess to shedding faith for anxiety
    and hope for worldly cynicism;
we have contaminated justice with prejudice,
    and mercy with conditional grace;
we have soured love with self-interest
    and humility with inverted pride;
we have debased your truth with our biases
    and your name with theological nit-picking;
we have diluted prayer with superstition
    and our worship with self-gratification.
Please forgive us all our infidelities
    and renew all that is pure and true within us.
Through Christ Jesus our Saviour.
    Amen!


*O my God, please send down on me from the clouds of your zeal the fiery love which will purify me of all that is not of you, that I may be worthy to praise you and able to love and serve you.*
*Adapted from Bahá'í Prayers, originally from Persia, 19th century*

**April 11**

*Pessimism is a grave infirmity of human minds. It is the bottomless*
*abyss between the ideal and the actual.*
P.T. Forsyth, theologian, England, 1848-1921

God of irrepressible new life,
you come on the wings of the morning
 and make light to shine
 on the just and the unjust.
Let the radiance of your love in Christ
 shine on every city, town, and farm house,
 that all over our land today
 folk may see the Light beyond light,
 and get a glimpse of your new world
 on which the sun never sets.
 Amen!

*Loving God,*
 *please strip away fear from us*
 *as the hunter strips skin from his kill.*
*Don't allow us to become anxious,*
 *but take each day as it comes.*
*Let our faith be as steady*
 *as a giant gum tree,*
 *and fierce as a desert wind,*
 *and as infectious as a child's chuckle.*
Author unknown – maybe Indigenous Australian

**April 12**

*What was good as our servant, becomes, as our master, evil; faith becomes fanaticism, mission becomes colonial colonization, communication turns into propaganda and education into indoctrination.*
  *Norman Young, minister and theologian, Australia, born 1930*

From dotting our theological *i's* and crossing our *t's*
    while neglecting the weighty deeds of mercy,
merciful God, deliver us.

From fulsome praying for the coming of your kingdom
    while in our daily affairs bowing down to Mammon,
merciful Christ, deliver us.

From seeking forgiveness for our own sins
    while nursing grudges against a neighbour,
merciful Spirit, deliver us.
Amen!

*Bless me, O God with a love of you, and of my neighbours. Give me peace of conscience, the command of my affections; and for the rest, your will be done! O king of peace, keep us in love and charity. Amen.*
  *Thomas Wilson, Bishop, Isle of Man, 1663-1755*

**April 13**

*There's summit as draws 'im uppards,*
*and summit as draws 'im down,*
*and consekence is 'e wobbles,*
*'twixt muck and a golden crown.*
        *G.A. Studdert Kennedy, poet and priest, England, 1883-1929*

Holy Friend,
others have sinned as I have sinned,
and for them I pray, as I do for myself,
that each of may recover the liberty
and the dignity of the children of God.

Blessed are you, Source of light and hope!
Blessed are you, Son of mercy and joy!
Blessed are you, Spirit of truth and empowerment!
Amen!

*You God, are father and mother to me, a brother, a sister, a friend*
*You manage my house for me. You care for all that are, and all that*
*are reside in you. We praise you and thank you, we give you glory,*
*human though we are and weak. You alone are God for all eternity!*
*Amen!*

                                    *Acts of Peter, c. 180*

**April 14**

*The higher the hill, the stronger the wind: so the loftier the life, the stronger the enemy's temptations.*
*John Wycliffe, Bible scholar, England, c. 1330-1384*

We pray, Awesome Friend,
    for your mercy upon our fractured nature.
We admit the deep-seated kink toward evil
    which leads us to act wilfully against you,
    against the happiness of our neighbours,
    and against even our own best interests.
O great Saviour of the world,
    by your grace please continue to liberate us from evil.
Enlighten our clouded minds and strengthen our weak wills,
    that we may begin to conquer where we once failed,
    and to spread good will where we once spread discord.
    For your love's sake.
    Amen!

*Be with me, Lord, at my rising in the morning. Have kindly regard to me, my Lord, and guide my actions, my words and my thoughts. Guide my hearing that I may pay no attention to gossip, and direct my feet that they may walk in your ways, and restrain my hands that they may have no truck with evil.*
*Book of Cerne, England, 10th century*

**April 15**

*When it comes your time to die, be not like those whose hearts are filled with the fear of death; sing your death song and die like a hero going home.*
*Attributed to Chief Tecumseh, Native American, Shawnee Nation,*
*USA, 1768-1813*

Blessed are you, wonder-full God,
     the up-surging Joy of the universe!
To us, you are and always will be:
     the voice that wakes the dead,
the sight that enlightens our eyes,
     the purpose that ingrains each day,
the loving that underpins faith,
     the delight that lifts us up
and that engenders compassion
     for family, neighbour and enemy.
Blessed are you, wonder-full God,
     you are the up-surging of all things.
Amen!

*You, who very early in the morning while the sun was arising, arose from the dead; raise us up daily unto newness of life, and save us, O our Lord and Saviour Jesus Christ.*
*Lancelot Andrewes, theologian, England, 1555-1626*

**April 16**

*The word 'Christianity' is a misnomer; in reality there has been only one Christian, and he died on the cross.*
*Friedrich Nietzsche, philosopher, Germany, 1844-1900*


Holy God, amazing Friend,
we are most grateful that long ago,
    on a bleak hill where men were executed,
    you forgave humanity its sin, defeated evil,
and with the precious blood of the Redeemer
    sealed a new covenant of grace, mercy and peace.
We thank you that we live in Christ's new, resurrection age,
    and neither our long-term faults, nor our short-term sins,
    can separate us from your untiring mercy and regeneration.
O Giver of life, lift up our despondent hearts!
O Redeemer of life, fill us with your peace!
O Renewer of life, infect us with your gladness.


*I may travel alone yet I'm never solitary, for you, my God, are always with me; there is no need to be afraid when the Lord of day and night is always here. Within your hand I am much safer than with an armed band.*
*Attributed to St. Columba, missionary, Iona, 521-597*

**April 17**

*Be a sinner and boldly, but more boldly have faith and rejoice in Christ.*

Martin Luther, protestant reformer, Germany, 1483-1546

Lord of indomitable faith,
of outrageous, abundant life,
of grace cascading upon grace,
    grant to each of us this morning
    a double measure of your Spirit
    and that love and joy which is indefatigable.
In your risen Name.
Amen!

*I confess to you, O God, that I do notice other people yet do not care about them enough. Please, in your loving kindness, supply my deficiency. Make me so to love all that I may be a blessing to all and please you in all that we may be knit together in godly love and united in your service. Amen!*

Thomas Traherne, poet-mystic, England, c. 1637-1674

**April 18**

*If you want others to be happy, practice compassion. If you want to be happy, practice compassion.*
*Attributed to the 14th Dalai Lama, Tibet and India, born 1935*

Most merciful God, our Liberator and holy Friend,
    please deliver us from all that is gloomy,
    and from everything that is stale and second rate.
Help us to return to you and recover
    those high spirits which come from loving
    and the tenacity which is grounded in faith,
withholding nothing from our commitment
    and permitting no barrier to stand in the way
    of your truth, mercy, peace and high spirits.
Through Christ Jesus our Saviour.
    Amen!

*Lord, rescue us from gloomy saints! Let your wisdom rule my entire life, that I may I gladly minister where and how you want me to. Please do not punish me by giving me the very things I want or beg for. Let me happily die to myself that I may better serve you, and to joyfully live in you who are the only true Life.*
*St. Teresa of Avila, nun and mystic, Spain, 1515-1582*

**April 19**

*Having ceased doubting him, I longed to experience Christ . . . It took about four months. It was like watching the sun rising very slowly. Suddenly I now knew it was real.*
              *Evelyn Underhill, author and mystic, England, 1875-1941*

Spirit of our risen Saviour, you can venture
        where no one else can go, and by-pass doors
        which our fears and anxieties try to keep closed;
Please open the dusty compartments of our hearts
        to the full inspection and cleansing
        of your invigorating Spirit of Truth;
Fling open the shutters of our minds
        that your sweet Breath may sweep away stagnation
        and fill us with your delightfulness.
Through Christ Jesus our Saviour,
        who is the very crucible of holy abundance.
Amen!

*O God, our Shepherd, give to the church a new vision and a new charity, new wisdom and fresh understanding, the revival of her brightness and the renewal of her unity; that the eternal message of your Son, undefiled by the traditions of men, may be hailed as the good news of the new age; through him who makes all things new, Jesus Christ our Lord.*
    *Percy Dearmer, Canon of Westminster Abbey, England, 1867-1936*

**April 20**

*It is on God alone that we can be sure that justice does not kill love
or love thwart justice.*

                    *P.T. Forsyth, theologian, England, 1848-1921*

We thank you, Holy Friend,
that your Eternal Christ
   comes among your people
    full of grace, and light and laughter.
Please infect us with his cheerfulness
   toughen us with his courage
   and sweeten us with his humility.
With the simplest, basic faith in him
   assist us to minister to our friends
   and do good to those who hate us;
For without his help we slip back
   into pre-Easter doubts and anxiety
   and miss the novelty of each day.
Amen!

*Big God; you come down to us from far above but also come up
from beneath us; from beyond the shining stars, but also from the
deep dust of our motherland. You hide yourself in the birds and
animals and send message-sticks in country and cloud. You come
near an' say "G'day" in brother Jesus, and show us that you're a
very good kind of God.*

                    *Attributed to an Indigenous Australian, date unknown*

**April 21**

*It is no more surprising to be born twice than once; everything in nature is resurrection.*

*Voltaire, philosopher and dramatist, France, 1694-1778*

God of Easter merriment, out of the grave
    you brought indomitable hope,
out of the dark tomb
    joyful liberation,
through the walls of despair
    came the dawn of endless day!
O beautiful are the wounded feet
    that carried good tidings of great joy
to all creatures great and small!
    Hallelujah Amen!

*O adorable and eternal God, through your crucified and risen Son you have made me a free agent, that I might become your friend. What a new fountain and torrent of joys you have prepared for us. O You who are so delightful to the children of earth, make me and other members of your family, delightful to you!*

*Adapted from Thomas Traherne, poet-mystic, England,*
*c. 1637-1674*

**April 22**


*The Depth that sings and dances within you is still dwelling within that first moment which scattered stars across the heavens.*
*Kahlil Gibran, poet, Lebanon, 1883-1931*


Creator of morning sunlight
    slanting through parklands
    and gilding avenues,
we praise you for this small reflection
    of that unexpected Living Light
bursting the bonds of death,
    resurrecting fallen faith,
and uplifting heavy hearts
    with unparalleled joy.
Marvellous are you,
    God of boundless new beginnings!
Amen!


*Thank you, my Creator and God, for giving me such a delight in your universe; this ecstasy when I look at your handiwork. As far as my finite sprit has been able to comprehend, I have shared with others the glory of your works and of your infinity. If anything I have said misrepresents you, or if at any time I have sought my own glory, graciously forgive me. Through Jesus Christ my Lord.*
*Johannes Kepler, pioneer astronomer, Germany, 1571-1630*

**April 23**

*Nature's music is never over; her silences are pauses, not conclusions.*
*Mary Webb, author, England, 1881-1927*

Should my best efforts
    seem rebuffed or appear wasted,
    keep me free from resentment
    or from drifting into pessimism.
Let me finish the course faithfully,
    go to my rest thankfully,
    sleep like a little child, deeply,
    and rise up again triumphantly.
Through Christ Jesus,
    my Brother, Saviour and Lord.
Amen!

*God, make each moment of our lives a miracle. God make us laugh*
*at the impossible. God give us hope when all seems hopeless, peace*
*where no peace could be, love for the unlovable. Make us gamble*
*on all your Almightiness, and dare everything in your great service.*
*Amen!*
*Adelaide E. Procter, poet, England, 1825-1864*

**April 24**

*At bottom, indeed, faith is a miracle. There is no denying it . . . it is the Gospel that creates in us the power to believe in the Gospel.*
                    *St. Augustine, Archbishop of Canterbury, England, c. 604*

O Joy of the whole universe,
let the excitement and young belief
    of Mary Magdalene
break in to the closed rooms
    where we house our doubts and defeats,
and shake up everything with the news
    that resurrection has happened
for all things and all people;
    even for me.
Amen!

*O God, who by the glorious death and resurrection of your Son has brought life and immortality to light; grant us so to die daily unto sin that we may ever live with you in the joy of the resurrection; through Jesus Christ to who be glory and dominion for ever and ever.*
                    *Gregorian Prayers – a compilation, Rome, c. 600*

**April 25  (Also see Appendix: Anzac Day)**

*There is not room for death, nor atom that Christ would render void; you are Being and Breath, and what you are may never be destroyed.*

*Emily Bronte, poet, England, 1818-1848*

Risen Lord Jesus,
you are the most blessed Enemy
    of our doubts and worries,
    of our fears and pessimisms;
you are the intolerant grace
    that breaks the bonds
    of constricting self-centeredness.
You are the hostile Word
    that assaults and shatters
    the hardening shell of apathy;
You, dearest enemy, truly you,
    are our healing and hope
    now and for all eternity.
Hallelujah!

*Praise be to you, God and Father of our Lord Jesus Christ, in your mercy you have given us new birth into a living hope by the resurrection of Jesus Christ from the dead. This inheritance into which you have given us new birth, is one that nothing can destroy or spoil or wither.*

*Attributed to the Apostle Peter*

**April 26**


*The influences that really make or mar human happiness are beyond the reach of the law. The law can keep neighbours from trespassing, but it cannot put neighbourly courtesy and goodwill into their relations.*
    *Walter Rauschenbusch, Baptist social activist, USA, 1861-1918*


This day, Risen Friend of the least and the last,
    we pray for those who experience
    the ache and fear of loss or loneliness.
May we not forget the need of
    the migrant, the orphan, the war-widow,
    the deserted wife or neglected husband,
    the unwanted teenager or spurned parent,
    and the defeated enemy.
Spirit of the truest friendship,
    draw from their hearts the ache,
    and give them your utter blessing and peace.
Amen!


*Magus, our dear little innocent child, now you are with the pure in heart in that lasting life that now is yours.*
*How full of joy you are now that your Mother in heaven has received you on returning from this mortal world!*
*O my heart, it is time to cease your mourning, and my eyes to cease their weeping.*
    *From a Christian epitaph, 3rd century*

**April 27**

*You [Jesus] stand among us*
*and all our defences*
*and reasons for unbelief*
*fall to the floor like old undies*
                    *Jennie Gordon, UCA minister and poet, Australia, born 1962*


Lord of the buoyant, Living Truth,
  please take your empty cross
     and use it like a mallet
     to crack open that hoary shell
of apathy or cynicism which too easily
corrodes and encrusts a weary faith.
     Break into our inner kernel of truth
     and liberate the songs of delight and joy
that are at risk of being consumed by cynicism,
and restore to us the delight of your salvation.
Amen!


*Make us more worthy, Lord, to serve our fellows throughout the*
*world who live and die in poverty and hunger. Give them, through*
*our hands, this day their daily bread. And by our understanding*
*love, give joy and peace. Amen!*
           *Attributed to Mother Teresa, religious sister and missionary,*
                                        *Calcutta, 1910-1997*

**April 28**

*When the Son of God is born in your heart then you have entered the fullness of time. He who has his heart established in the eternal Christ, in him is the fullness of time.*
*Meister Eckhart, author and mystic, Germany, 1260-1328*

Keep watch, Emmaus Friend,
    with those who travel a lonely road,
    or watch by a dear one's bedside,
and give your guardian angels care
    of those who soundly sleep.
Nurse your sick children,
    rest your weary ones,
comfort your dying ones,
    soothe you suffering ones,
shield your little ones,
    and encourage your aged ones;
all for your love's sake. Amen!
*In the mood of St. Augustine, Bishop of Hippo, North Africa,*
*354-430*

*Author of all marvels, we praise you. Creator of all things heavenly and earthly, we praise you. Your power and your wisdom are everywhere displayed. You have placed the night skies to be a roof over our heads, and the solid and fruitful earth to be the ground under our feet. O Father and Guardian of humankind, we thank and praise you! Amen!*
*Based on Caedmon, Christian poet, Northumbria, 6th century*

**April 29**

*We still feel at times that your loving concern for others might cost us too dearly, so we hold back and withdraw.*
           Ron Gordon, UCA minister and writer, Australia, born 1932

God of the pure and the poor,
    let the peace of your tomb-emptying Son
rest with special grace and beauty
    on your dearly loved native peoples.
Guide those who are strong in spirit
    to give wise and bold leadership.
Channel the anger of the desperate
    into creative plans for reform.
Surround with your deep comfort
    those who are broken and lost.
And in your mercy,
    send a modern Jonah to the rest of us
lest we perish in our blindness.
Amen!

*We pray, O Lord, to direct and guide your church with your unfailing care, that it may be diligent in times of quiet, and daring in times of trouble. Through Jesus Christ our Lord.*
                         Franciscan breviary, Italy, c. 1226

**April 30**

*You never enjoy the world aright, till it is as if the sea itself is flowing in your veins, until you feel yourself clothed with the heavens and washed with the stars!*
                    Thomas Traherne, poet-mystic, England, c. 1637-1674

Joy! Sunrise faith, Mary's joy!
      Fear flees, despair dies; Christ is risen indeed!
Let the trees of the forest clap their hands,
      let city streets and parklands rejoice,
let the mountains and hills skip for joy,
      let town houses and towers celebrate,
let the dingo and the lamb dance together,
      let towns and remote farms celebrate,
let the child lead the calf and the lion,
      let cathedrals and chapels sing their praises,
let the earth be full of the joy of the Lord
      like the tossing waves of the sea!
Joy! Sunrise faith, Mary's joy!
      I live, yet not I, for Christ lives in me!
Christ is risen indeed!
Hallelujah!

*Lord, make me like a crystal, that your light may shine through me. Amen!*
                    Katherine Mansfield, writer, New Zealand and England,
                                                      1888-1923

**May 1**


*What else can I do, a weak old man, but sing hymns of joy to God? If I were a lark, I would do it with song. If I were a crane, I would do it with elegant dance. But I am a rational creature, and I ought to praise God with my mind and speech, as well as with heart and soul.*

*Epictetus, stoic philosopher, Rome, c. 60-130*

Holy, risen Lord Jesus,
    teach me to fear you without being afraid,
    to love you without being pretentious,
to serve you with style and tenacity
    without becoming heavy-laden or servile,
    and to adore you, holding nothing back.
Through the Name that is above all other names,
    my sure confidence and good health.
    Amen!


*Lord, there are beggars who, even in midsummer go to sleep hungry, and who in winter are poor, wet-shod wanderers: frozen, famished and foully tested, yet who are berated by the rich who have no time to listen. O Lord Christ, comfort your careworn folk; Bless them, Christ, with your riches. Send them a summer of happiness. Amen.*

*Based on poem of William Langland, poet, England, c. 1332 – c. 1400*

**May 2**

*The possession of riches is not for ever. The splendour of beauty does not last. Physical strength soon withers away, and all our boasting is so much smoke and emptiness.*
*Apostolic Constitutions, Syria, c. 375-380*

Merciful God, forgive both our sins and our follies,
 those of which we are excruciatingly aware
 and those that are hiding behind pride and fears.
Please bathe us, heal us, reinvigorate us,
 for without your saving loveliness
 the final story-line of our life
will be one of misread situations,
 many missed opportunities,
 and misused time and ability.
Through Christ Jesus, our source of life and love.
Amen!

*Look at me, O God, and deal with my jealousy. I confess there are times when I would rather your work not done than to see another do it better than I could perform it. Forgive me, loving God, and dispossess me of this evil demon. Please give me humility to learn from others, not to conceitedly outshine them but to see more of your will done on earth, as it is in heaven. For you name's sake.*
*Abbreviated from Thomas Fuller, historian, England, 1608-1661*

**May 3**

*To be satisfied with a little, is the greatest wisdom; and he that increases his riches, increases his worries; but a contented mind is a hidden treasure, and troubles cannot afflict it.*
                    *Pharaoh Akhenaton, monotheist, Egypt, c. 1300 BC*

A yellow-breasted robin
    perches sideways on the trunk
of a stringy-bark tree
    and watches us eat lunch,
    hoping for a handout.
When we throw some crumbs,
    he spends more time
    chasing other birds away
than actually eating.
    My God,
He's almost human!

*Blessed are You for people who believe in peace and love, despite 'the facts'; who keep the faith within in this harsh world, and who never hide from the light; those nameless saints who are ready to suffer for the sake of your new age of light, love and holy merriment.*
    *Huub Oosterhuis, theologian, poet and social activist, Netherlands,*
                                                              *born 1933*

**May 4**

*To be willing to change your mind and to follow him who has set you right is to actually become the free agent that you thought you were.*

*Helen Keller, deaf-blind social activist, USA, 1880-1968*

Deliver us, God of Easter liberty,
    from silly pride and stubbornness
    in days of success and prosperity,
    in failure and uncertainty,
    in times of disease or tragedy,
    and in heartbreak and death.
Holy God, Saviour of those who know you,
and of those who as yet know you not,
    please never tire of us, never give up on us,
    for only in your service is found perfect freedom,
    healing peace, and unadulterated delight.
Though Christ Jesus our Redeemer.
    Amen!

*Eternal God,*
*may we all live by faith and walk in hope,*
*and be renewed by love and grace*
*until the wide world reflects your glory,*
*and you are all in all to all.*

*Traditional prayer, England*

**May 5**

*Who is a holy person? One who is aware of the suffering of others and does something about it.*
*Kabir, mystic and poet, India, c. 1440 – c. 1518*

It shakes us up, loving God,
    whenever we visit a friend in Intensive Care.
Normally we are insulated against
    critical accidents and illness,
    but suddenly, here we are, face to face.
Bless, we pray you,
    all this complex medical technology,
    the skill and compassion of nurses
    and of physicians' hands and brains.
Beyond all else, God,
    please give to this, and every such patient,
    be they known to us or unknown,
that unique intensive care
    of your own Healing Spirit.
Amen!

*Lord, my soul is in a chill, dry land, all dried up and cracked by the strength of the cold north wind. But whatever you see as the best for me is good enough; I ask for nothing more. You will send me both dew and warmth when it pleases you; Amen.*
*Jane de Chantal, founder of a new religious order, France,*
*1572-1641*

**May 6**

*A religious person who professes to climb higher than he can in fact achieve, possesses the name of sanctity without substance, because in name alone, without a structure of good works, he glories in a kind of vain ecstasy of the mind.*
                    *Attributed to Abbess Hildegard of Bingen, mystic-composer,*
                                                    *Germany, 1098-1179*

For this morning's activity in this busy city,
and the varied gifts and skills
        of those thousands of minds and hands
cooperating in the work and opportunity
        of this one unrepeatable day,
we give you our hearty thanks,
        O God of the city.
Through Christ Jesus;
        Amen!

*We worship you, O God, lover of humanity, as we set before you our weakness that you may replace it with your strength. We pray for the afflicted, the captives, the poor, and the frail and sick. Strengthen them, rescue them from bondage, deliver them from wretchedness, and console every one. Through your only-begotten Son, Jesus Christ; Amen.*
                        *Serapion, Bishop of Thmuis, Egypt, c. 350*

**May 7**


*Happiness is not some state of being to arrive at, rather it is a manner of travelling.*
                         *Dr. Samuel Johnson, scholar, England, 1709-1784*



Save us, Holy Friend,
     from living on the wrong side of Easter.
Rescue us from those acidic doubts
     which eat away at our optimism;
and from the malaise that is bred and fed
     by a lack of commitment to hope and love.
Return us to the radiant clarity
     of trusting you unconditionally.
Open our eyes to the beauty of wild flowers
     and the freedom of wild ravens,
which can do nothing but rely on you
     for the necessities of life.
Through Jesus brother and Saviour. Amen!



*You, who fill heaven and earth, always busy, always quiet, who are present everywhere and everywhere are fully present; You who are not absent when far away, who with your whole being fill yet go beyond all things; You who teach the hearts of the faithful without the din of words, teach us, we pray. Through Jesus Christ our Lord. Amen!*
                    *St. Augustine, Bishop of Hippo, North Africa, 354-430*

**May 8**

*If you are at home at 9.00 am, noon, or 3.00 pm, immediately say
aloud your prayers and praises to God. But if you are elsewhere at
this moment, pause and silently praise God in your heart.*
                    *Hippolytus, reformer and Bishop, Rome, c. 170 – c. 236*

Out of the gloom of primeval fears
    arose resilient hope and faith,
out of the cold tomb of grief
    came liberation and laughter,
through the walls of utter despair
    walked the light of endless day,
O beautiful upon the mountains
    are the running feet of Mary
who brings good tidings of deathless love,
    'I have seen the Lord!'
Hallelujah!

*Come, Lord Jesus, and do 'your love thing' among us, set us on fire
and clasp us close; draw us to your loveliness. Let us love, let us run
to you and for you. Amen.*
                    *St. Augustine, Bishop of Hippo, North Africa, 354-430*

**May 9**

*The Kingdom of God is not a matter of getting individuals to heaven,
but of transforming the life on earth into the harmony of heaven.*
       *Walter Rauschenbusch, Baptist social activist, USA, 1861-1918*

Christ, you are risen in deed!
    With you alive beside us we are now bold to say:
blessed are the meek, the poor, the hungry and grieving,
blessed are the merciful, the pure and the abused.

And in so saying, Loving God,
    we pledge ourselves to do all that we can
to bring this kingdom of new values and goals
into the living of our community and nation.
        Christ, you are risen in deed!
        Hallelujah!

*Eternal God, you wrap us in love both night and day. Please lift the
curtain of darkness from the world and burn away the fog from our
hearts. Rise up with the morning sun and shine upon our souls, and
make lively all our work and our prayer. Amen.*
            *James Martineau, Unitarian scholar, France, 1805-1900*

**May 10**

*The great Spirit is in all things . . . in trees, grasses rivers, mountains, animals and winged creatures, people; and even more important this One is above all these things.*

Attributed to Black Elk, Native American, USA, 1863-1950

O Joy of the universe!
Your majesty, our smallness;
your meekness, our arrogance;
your wisdom, our ignorance;
your eternity, our mortality;
your loveliness, our gracelessness;
your inexorable loving, our adoration.
Yes Lord, Yes!
Hallelujah!

*We beseech you, O living Lord, for the peace that is from above to spread everywhere: in our houses and our families that they may be wholesome, in our pastors, teachers and governors that they may be diligent, in our cities, towns and countryside, that all may be harmonious; and for all that travel by land, air and sea that each may reach their destination in peace and good will. Amen!*

St. John Chrysostom, Archbishop of Constantinople, Rome,
c. 347-407

**May 11**

*Have a heart that never hardens, and a temper that never tires, and a touch that never hurts.*
*Charles Dickens, novelist, England, 1812-1870*

Abba-God, bless all church families
 with the gift of generosity,
  that the love we share together
  in the security of your house
may set us free of self
 to love our neighbours
 and pray for our enemies.
In the spirit of Jesus,
 our brother and Lord,
Amen!

*O God, may we so live that our world may not be ravished by our greed nor spoiled by our ignorance. May we hand on earth's common heritage of life, undiminished in joy when our bodies return in peace to You, our Great Mother who has nourished them.*
*Walter Rauschenbusch, Baptist social activist, USA, 1861-1918*

**May 12**

*You need to be de-intellectualized. I believe you ought to get yourself, gently and gradually, interested in the poor; you should visit and help them, quietly and unostentatiously.*
*Baron von Hügel, spiritual director, Austria and England,*
*1852-1925*

In home, school, workplace, and on the web;
    between races, religions, and nations;
help us, strong and merciful God,
    to put an end to hostility
    and every form of bullying.
Teach us, from childhood to old age,
    better ways of handling fears and hurts,
    and of dealing with conflict when it arises.
Give us the humble, stick-at-it love
    of the Prince of Peace.
Amen!

*How thankful I am, O God, that you know me better than I know myself, and you allow me to know myself better than those around me. Please make me, I beg you, better than others think I am, and forgive me the evil they do not know.*
*Amen.*
*Attributed to Abu Bekr, mystic, Syria, c. 620*

**May 13**

*What is THIS that gleams through me and smites my heart without wounding it so that I am both a-shudder and a-glow.*
*St. Augustine, Bishop of Hippo, North Africa, 354-430*

Though our lips should speak with the innocence of infants,
    or with a skill outstripping Shakespeare,
our tongues sing with the high spirits of lyrebirds
    or with the harmonies of Mozart,
our minds become enlightened with holy intuitions
    far beyond speech or song,
and our eyes shine with a love as serene as moonlight
    yet as bright as a summer sunrise,
though we should join with one massed choir
    from all the nations of earth –
Yet, we would not even have begun to worthily praise you,
    God of Christ Jesus.

*Holy One, If I should worship you because I am afraid of hell, then burn me in hell! If I should worship you to get into paradise, then exclude me from paradise. But if I worship you just for your own sake, do not withhold from me your everlasting beauty.*
*Attributed to Rabia the Sufi, Persia, 8th century*

**May 14**

*Whoever fails to recognise in the marred visage of any social derelict the image of Him who was despised and rejected of man . . . can have no place among the Architect's workmen.*
                    *Joseph Furphy, novelist, Australia, 1843-1912*


Somewhere, right now, today
    someone is getting prepped
    to go to the operating theatre.
Please give her (or him) a calm mind
    and a serene confidence
    in your absolute Presence.
Guide the skills of the anaesthetist,
    steady the eyes and hands of the surgeons,
    bless the disciplined care of the nurses,
and through the brooding Holy Spirit,
    grant the gift of healing.
In the name the Wounded Healer,
    Jesus Christ our Saviour.
Amen!


*Lord, school me in the art of patience while I am in good health, and show me how to employ such patience when I become ill. When the bad times come, either put some more backbone into me or lighten my burden. As in my strength I have proved much weakness, then in my weakness may I prove your strength.*
                    *Thomas Fuller, historian, England, 1608-1661*

**May 15**

*Though by day my feet are palsied and my days are boring, in my sleep at night I go flying and soaring.*
*Anonymous, ancient Chinese, date unknown*

Implant us, dear Lord
with that post-Easter miracle
which can transform setbacks into growth,
    suffering into faith,
and sorrows into healing tears
    of utter wonder and delight.
Amen!

*God, is not our eyesight a jewel? Is not hearing a treasure? Is not speech a glory? O my Lord, pardon my ingratitude, when in my dullness I am not alert to these gifts. These things are so close to me that I have taken them for granted. You have gifted me with many blessings and I am not aware. But now I give thanks and adore you for all your inestimable favours.*
*Thomas Traherne, poet-mystic, England, c. 1637-1674*

**May 16**

*Jesus is the Light of the World, yet he ministers like a menial servant at the feet of these little, foolish fishermen and tax-gatherers. What do you think moved me but just this huge, life-and-love-bringing paradox; here is its fullest, humblest activity?*
                    *Baron von Hügel, spiritual director, Austria and England,*
                                                            *1852-1925*


Source of life and love,
    we know that we are being raised up,
not through own hard-won worthiness,
    but because in the Son of Man
you have called us out of darkness
    and named us your children of light.
Amen!


*A Presence that disturbs me with the joy*
*Of elevated thoughts; a sense sublime*
*Of something far more deeply interfused,*
*Whose dwelling is the light of setting suns,*
*And the round ocean, and the living air,*
*And the blue sky, and in the mind of man,*
*A motion and a spirit, that impels*
*All thinking things, all objects of all thought,*
*And rolls through all things.*
                    *William Wordsworth, poet, England, 1770-1850*

**May 17**

*Lord, enable me to see your glory in every place. If earthly beauty sets my soul alight, then it shall seem a mere candle compared to your luminous grace.*
*Michelangelo, painter-sculptor, Italy, 1475-1564*

God most wonderful, I want to praise you more. Not because you are some divine egomaniac who needs our pitiful flattery to keep you in a good mood. O no, never that!

Let me praise you because the more I think about your goodness the more I delight in, cherish and love you; and to love you fully has become the chief goal of my life.

So, my most blessed Friend, may I never cease from pondering the variety of your goodness, neither now nor in the eternity which lies ahead of me.

Amen!

*Lord, make me know you truly, that I may ever more love, enjoy and possess you. And since in this mortal life I cannot fully attain this blessing, let it at least grow within me day by day, until it can be fulfilled at last in the life that is to come.*
*St. Anselm, Archbishop of Canterbury, England, 1033-1109*

**May 18**

*I hunger to hear*
*the voice of creation*
*calming the chaos*
*and claiming each child*
          *Jennie Gordon, UCA minister and poet, Australia, born 1962*

God of resurgent life,
    give new life to our first citizens
    from Darwin to Hobart,
    and from Broome to Sydney.
May the risen Friend
    be among them with great love,
sharing their frustration and prayers,
    and giving them the will
    to claim that better future
which you alone can give us all.

*O Worker of the universe, we pray to you to let the irresistible*
*current of your universal energy come like the impetuous warm*
*wind of spring; let it come rushing over the vast field and the life of*
*humanity; let it bring the scent of many flowers, the murmuring of*
*many woodlands; let it make sweet and vocal the lifelessness of our*
*dried up soul-life. Let our newly awakened powers cry for unlimited*
*fulfilment in leaf and flower and fruit, for you.*
          *Rabindranath Tagore, poet, India, 1861-1941*

**May 19**


*It is not the rigidity of material or mathematical determinism that gives the universe consistency, but the subtle works of the Spirit.*
          *Teilhard de Chardin, priest-scientist-mystic, France, 1881-1955*



Soft as the breath
    of the risen Lord,
breathing forgiveness
    as gift and vocation
    on his gathered disciples,
Spirit of mercy, move
    on each of us;
let us inhale deeply
    of the very breath
    of your irrepressible life.
Amen!



*I adore you, Lord Jesus, dwelling in my heart. I beseech you abide in me, in all the tranquillity of your power, in all the perfection of your ways, in all the brightness of your presence and in all the holiness of your Spirit; that I may know the breadth and length and depth and height of your love; and do, please, trample down in me all power of evil in the might of your Spirit, to the glory of God the Father.*
          *Jean-Jacques Olier, priest, France, 1608-1657*

**May 20**


*When you tread the earth with me*
*the light is clear before me*
*and my spirit, too, is free.*
*Henry Lawson, poet, Australia, 1867-1922*


Inflowing Joy,
    the Soul of outgoing love,
you come among us
    with the quietest power.
You mend our brokenness
    and nurture the roots
of our very being.
    Awesome is you presence!
Wonderful is your name,
    Spirit of truth,
the gift from Christ Jesus!
Amen!


*Almighty God, by the gift of your Spirit please establish and ground*
*us in your truth. Reveal to us what we need to know, perfect us in*
*what is lacking, strengthen in us what we do know, and keep us in*
*your service without fault. Through Jesus Christ our Lord. Amen!*
*Clement, Bishop of Rome, died c. 99*

**May 21**

*Christian optimism refuses to bow to present disasters. It enables a man to hold his head high, to claim the future for himself and not to abandon it to the enemy.*
   *Dietrich Bonhoeffer, theologian and martyr, Germany, 1906-1945*

Breath forgiving,
Fire remoulding,
Wind all-cleansing:
     make us utterly yours,
     heirs of light and laughter
     and the children of liberty.
Beautiful are your ways,
Holy Spirit, Awesome Friend,
     in all the universe
     throughout time and eternity.
     Hallelujah!

*Strengthen me, O God, by the grace of your Holy Spirit. Grant me to be empowered with inner strength, and to empty my heart of all useless care and anguish. O Lord, grant me heavenly wisdom, that I may learn above all things to relish and love you, and to think of other things as being, as indeed they are, at the disposal of your providence. Amen.*
   *Thomas à Kempis, scholar, Germany, 1380-1471*

**May 22**

*Holy is the Spirit present to Jesus, aiding his encounters with human need, and helping him cope with the resistance of human misrepresentation.*

*Ron Gordon, UCA minister and writer, Australia, born 1932*

You are always at work, Spirit of Truth:
You bring beauty out of chaos,
meaning out of hazard and chance,
and new life out of decay and death.

You bubble up within us like a refreshing spring,
energizing your church to employ the love of Jesus
in all our coming together in worship and fellowship
and at our going out as Christ's servant people in the world.

Blessed are you, Sister Spirit of truth,
right now and evermore!
Amen!

*May your servants, O God, be set on fire with your spirit, strengthened by your power, illumined by your splendour, filled with your grace, and led forward with your aid; and having courageously finished our course, may we be embraced happily in your eternal kingdom.*
*Amen.*

*Gallican Prayers, France, 9th century*

**May 23**

*It is difficult for a woman to define her feelings in language which is chiefly made by men to express theirs.*
                              *Thomas Hardy, novelist, England, 1840-1928*


Sister Spirit, sweet Counsellor,
    your patience is awesome.
I am cantankerous and foolish,
    but you don't leave me,
I am fickle and disloyal,
    but you don't leave me,
I am rude and arrogant,
    but you don't leave me,
I am anxious, humourless, faithless,
    but you don't leave me.
Sister Spirit, awesome Counsellor,
    thanks for being here for me.
Amen!


*Tune me, O God, in to one glorious harmony with you; into one responsive, vibrant chord; that we might offer you all thanks and melody, all love and praise. For this joy, please tune me, O loving Lord.*
                              *Attributed to Christina Rossetti, poet, England, 1830-1894*

**May 24**

*How could I ever presume to complain, about my many needs, when I possess so great a treasure chest in Christ Jesus.*
                    Symeon, the New Theologian, Constantinople, 949-1022

God, our wonderful Pentecost Spirit,
    how glorious is your name
    in all the earth!
We celebrate with bubbling joy
    the new age of hope and joy,
    this new time of opportunity,
Things trodden down
    are being raised up;
things growing old
    are being made young;
all things are returning
    to their premised perfection,
and glorious is your name
    among the children of light,
Amen!

*O eternal God, who has taught us by your holy word that our bodies are the temples of your Spirit, keep us we most humbly ask you, temperate and holy in thought, word and deed, that at the last we, with all the pure in heart, may see you, and be made like you in your heavenly kingdom, through Christ our Lord, Amen.*
                    Brooke Foss Westcott, Bishop of Durham, England, 1825-1901

**May 25**

*Quietly as rosebuds*
  *talk to the thin air*
*Love came so lightly*
  *I knew not he was there*

*Shaw Neilson, poet, Australia, 1872-1942*


Shake us up, Awesome Friend,
    and deliver us from losing our souls
    under the babble of today's technology,
With our busy laptops, smartphones and iPads,
    with googling and twittering, texting and Skype,
where is there even a tiny space of time
    for us to listen to your 'still, small voice of calm'?

Saviour Christ, come and rescue us from ourselves
    that we, like the Prodigal Son, may come to our senses,
and make time to return home to where we truly belong,
    in the joy and fellowship of your Holy Spirit.
Amen!


*Loving God, you have decided to restore all things to their intended glory in your beloved son, Jesus. Grant that we and all nations, fractured as we are by evil, may be brought under the gentle yoke of his most loving rule; who with you and the Holy Spirit, live and love, forever one God. world without end.*

*Salisbury Prayers, England, c. 1100*

**May 26**

*The Spirit will flow free, high surging where she will,*
*in prophet's words she spoke of old, today speaks still.*
*Medieval doxology*

Forgive us, merciful God,
for daring to presume
　　that through our piety
　　we could ever domesticate
　　your Holy Spirit.
Come upon us again
with the sovereign liberty
　　that is like a rushing wind
　　and as tongues of fire;
Bring us on our knees
　　with that wonder and awe
　　which is the beginning of wisdom,
and to that lifestyle
　　which is faith expressed by love.
Amen!

*O God, who has taught us to fulfil all your commandments by loving*
*you and our neighbour: Grant us the grace of your Holy Spirit, that*
*we may be devoted to you with our whole heart and united to each*
*other with a pure affection; through Jesus Christ our Lord.*
*Leonine Prayers, Rome, 5th century*

**May 27**


*I will pour out my Spirit on all people; Your old people shall dream dreams and your young folk shall see visions.*
                    *Joel ben Pethuel, prophet, ancient Israel, c. 600 BC*



That we may be
    young enough to see visions,
    yet old enough to dream dreams,
move freely, Spirit-Friend,
    and enlist us in the service
    of Christ's new age.
For your love's sake;
Amen!



*How is it I can embrace You within myself, yet see you spread across the infinite heavens? You know how. You alone. You, who made this mystery. You who shine like the sun within my breast. You, although immaterial, yet shine in my material heart. You alone know how.*
                    *Symeon, the New Theologian, Constantinople, 949-1022*

**May 28**

*When you sincerely say a prayer, the Holy Spirit is in every word of it, and like a Holy Fire, penetrates each syllable.*
                    *John of Kronstadt, priest and mystic, Russia, 1829-1908*


Holy Spirit, we thank you for the gift of the breath of peace,
    but also for the less comfortable gift of your fire.
Blessed is the fire that burns yet does not consume,
    that thaws frigid souls and exposes them to love.
Blessed the fire that welcomes weary pilgrims at evening,
    and for the warmth that gathers opposites into community.
And blessed also is the furnace that softens steely hearts,
    bends wills into new patterns of beauty and usefulness,
    and, where needful, melts down the arrogant spirit
    to patiently begin to shape our lives all over again.
Thank you, Spirit of Christ Jesus and our God.
Amen!


*God of all goodness, inspire us to desire you passionately, to seek you astutely, to know you confidently and to serve you flawlessly, to the glory of your holy name. Amen.*
                    *Thomas Aquinas, theologian and philosopher, Italy, 1224-1274*

**May 29**

*We know not the matter of the things for which we should pray, neither the object to whom we pray, nor the medium by or through whom we pray; none of these things know we: but by the help and assistance of the Spirit.*
        *John Bunyan, Puritan preacher and author, England, 1628-1688*

Holy Spirit, our Companion,
    the life-blood of sincere prayer,
    the soul of melody and spirit of harmony,
    the most intimate Presence of God:
we worship and praise you,
we want to love and serve you
    with that blessed servitude
    that flows from the pure liberty
    of being the joint-heirs of Christ,
and with the love that is inspired
    by the cross and empty tomb,
    in the life that is abundantly rich.
Amen!

*O God, renew our spirits by your Holy Spirit, and draw our hearts to yourself, that our work may not be a burden but a delight. Let us not serve you like slaves under the spirit of bondage but with freedom and gladness as your children, rejoicing in fulfilling your will; for Jesus Christ's sake.*
        *Benjamin Jenks, pastor and writer, England, 1646-1724*

**May 30**

*And my dreams are wild dreams, and old dreams are new;*
*They haunt me and daunt me with fears of tomorrow;*
*My brothers they doubt me, but my dreams come true.*
                    Henry Lawson, poet, Australia, 1867-1922


Please, Spirit of the living God,
neither allow the grand visions of the young
        to wilt, wither and decay
        in the drought of secular cynicism,
nor permit the dreams of the old folk
        to retreat into a fanciful nostalgia
        for the 'good old days.'
May the old still retain, and deliver in action,
        the youthful spirit of Jesus,
and the young inherit and practice with impunity
        the vision of the pure in heart.
In the name of Father, Son and the Holy Spirit.
        Amen!


*Breathe on me, O God, with the Spirit that infuses energy and*
*kindles fervour. In asking for fervour I am asking for more faith,*
*hope and love, and for feelings that issue in service. In asking for*
*energy I am asking that as long as I draw breath my life will be*
*dedicated to trying to do the best I can with the gifts you have given*
*me. Amen.*
        *Inspired by John Henry Newman, Cardinal, England and Ireland,*
                                        *1801-1890*

**May 31**

*The soul must stop gadding about everywhere. She must learn to stay at home in her inmost self, for there God is present and always near.*
              *Meister Eckhart, author and mystic, Germany, 1260-1328*

Spirit of Christ Jesus, please attune us to:
      the forgotten love-songs of your kingdom,
      the healing medicine of your kindly hands,
      the listening that hears the unspoken words,
      the eyes that read what is hidden in hearts;
and align us with the unique love that is content to carry
      whatever burden, shame or cross
      which faith, hope and love may require.
Amen!

*Sweet Jesus, I thank you with all my heart for that sweet sounding prayer you made before your sacred passion on the Mountain of Olives: Not my will but yours be done. Teach me, sweet Jesus, to be ever ready to do your will, for when my will lines up with yours, that is true happiness.*
              *Richard Rolle, mystic, England, c. 1300-1349*

**June 1**

*often I have been bewildered by your*
*silence*
*in this sea of chaos on which our*
*little boat*
*struggles to keep afloat*
                *Jennie Gordon, UCA minister and poet, Australia, born 1962*


When troubles swarm around us
    like a hive of bees,
and fears rise within us
    like a plague of locusts,
come, Counsellor- Spirit,
    and be to us as a shield without
and the purest light
    of common sense within.
Through Christ Jesus;
    Amen!


*O Lord, my God, the light of the blind and strength of the weak; yet*
*much more than that. You are also the light of those who see and*
*the strength of the strong. Please listen to the my soul crying from*
*its deep places, for we know you are here in our hearts when we*
*throw ourselves upon you, and weep in your arms. After all our*
*rugged ways, you gently wipe away our tears. Then we weep the*
*more for sheer joy, because you so remake and comfort us.*
                *St. Augustine, Bishop of Hippo, North Africa, 354-430*

**June 2**

*Cheerfulness, it would appear, is a matter which depends fully as much on the state of things within us, as on the state of things without and around us.*

*Charlotte Bronte, writer, England, 1816-1855*

Holy Spirit, you are the fountain of purest joys:
    the spring of playfulness which underlies serious moments,
of the good humour that outsoars our stumbling,
    of the smiles that can surface out of tragedy,
and the one who can bestow,
    even in the valley of the shadow of death,
the triumphant gift of Divine comedy.

Glorious are you, our truth and counsellor,
    playmate, regenerator, guiding light,
the vine bearing the very fruits of heaven,
    best friend, workmate, brother,
and the holy merriment that will one day fill,
    consume and complete all things.
Hallelujah!

*I testify, O my God, that if I were given a thousand lives by you, and offered them up all in your path, I would still have failed to repay the least of the gifts which, by your grace, you have freely bestowed upon me.*

*Adapted from Bahá'í Prayers, originally from Persia, 19th century*

**June 3**

*We dare not reduce humanity to the limited proportions of our own experience and imagination. You see, Christ's difference from us, shows both his divinity and the perfection of his humanity.*
*David Beswick, UCA minister and psychologist, Australia, born 1933*

Holy Spirit, regenerator of big possibilities,
    thank you for your patient nurturing of my soul.
Please continue to shape my becoming,
    dig down deeply into my hidden-ness;
help germinate seeds that have been dormant,
    encourage tendrils that stretch up for more light;
toughen growth that must face coming storms,
    prune old growth that has served its purpose;
and hasten the day when I shall have changed
    more into the likeness of your beautiful Son.
Amen!

*We praise you, Christ Jesus, for the perfume of happiness that is pouring upon us as we receive your light. Already we are gathering spiritual flowers and plaiting crowns fit for heaven. Already the Spirit has breathed her fragrance upon us and we already are standing in the outer courts of your royal palace!*
*Cyril, Bishop of Jerusalem, theologian, c. 313 – c. 386*

**June 4**

*Christ's courage was one that rested on love rather than on strength.*
*It was in loving that his strength to be independent was grounded.*
                    *P.T. Forsyth, theologian, England, 1848-1921*


O Spirit of true vision,
     when our steps seem small
     and the mountain peaks far off,
save us from indulgent self-pity
     and deliver us from rank defeatism.
Let us be thankful
     that in spite of poor eyesight
we have truly glimpsed
     the delectable mountains,
and give us satisfaction and joy
     in every stride forwards
and each small step upwards.
For your love's sake.
Amen!


*Stir us up to offer you, O Lord, our bodies, our mind, in all we love*
*and all we learn, in all we plan and do, to offer our labours, our*
*pleasures, our sorrows to you; to work through them for your*
*Kingdom; to live as those who are not their own but are bought*
*with your blood, fed with your body; yours from our birth-hour,*
*yours now, and yours for ever and ever.*
               *Charles Kingsley, minister and social reformer, England,*
                                             *1819-1875*

## June 5

*What I do unto one of the least of these my brothers I do unto Christ. But what if the very least and worst of all people, is me? Will I then love and cherish myself as I would Christ?*
*Inspired by Karl Jung, psychotherapist, Switzerland, 1875-1961*

Holy Friend, please nurture within our private being
    a pure and good humoured love of ourselves;
Not that brand of ugly self-love
    which is rooted in arrogance or gross selfishness,
but a love which treasures and nurtures
    the unique spirit you have made each one of us.
For in loving ourselves you set us free to love others
    with neither competitive jealousy nor judgement,
just as in your true-man Jesus
    you have first so superbly loved us.
Amen!

*Give me, O God, the Spirit of wisdom and understanding, the Spirit of counsel and strength, the Spirit of knowledge, godliness, and of your awe. Make me ever to seek your face with all my heart, all my soul, all my mind; grant me to have a contrite and humble heart in your Presence.*
*Gallican Prayers, France, c. 6th century*

**June 6**

*I have no time to be in a hurry.*
*John Wesley, clergyman and evangelist, England, 1703-1791*


More, much more
  to learn and cherish you
to relish and serve you
  and to adore you evermore;
this is our deepest soul-yearning,
  dearest Companion-Spirit!
Amen!


*As the first light strokes*
*finger-pink across horizon's brow*
  *I ask you now*
*to bless my feet with courage*
  *that I may walk on*
*to bless my hands with gentleness*
  *so that my touch may be light*
*to bless my mouth with wisdom*
  *so that I make speak life*
*and to bless my heart with love*
  *so that I may pour your blessing*
*on all we meet*
*in this dawning day*
  *Jennie Gordon, UCA minister and poet, Australia, born 1962*

**June 7**

*God the Father is a deep root, the Son is the shoot that breaks forth into the world, and the Spirit is that flower which spreads beauty and fragrance.*

*Tertullian, lawyer and scholar, Africa, c. 155-220*

O God, our Creator, constantly
    you renew the face of the earth;
    we worship and adore you,
O God, our Saviour, constantly
    you renew our broken, soiled lives;
    we worship and adore you,
O God, our Spirit Friend, constantly
    you renew the life of the church;
    we worship and adore you.
Amen!

*Make me a worthy temple of your Spirit; no more a temple of sin but a child of light. You alone are the true radiance of souls, and to you, as God and Master, we give all glory every single day of our lives.*

*Symeon, the New Theologian, Constantinople, 949-1022*

**June 8**

*To deal with contemporary mood of weariness, amounting in some cases to despair, pessimism, and nihilism, we must have something greater than an ambition of our own. We need a God, in brief, one who is at the same time the Mighty One and our Humble Redeemer.*
*P.T. Forsyth, theologian, England, 1848-1921*

Another cold, slate-grey evening:
    perched on the pinnacle of a pencil pine:
one delightfully absurd, common blackbird,
    its taut throat thrust upwards
sends out a love melody into the gloom;
    such defiant joy overwhelms me.
I bow three times in glad homage
    to the Composer;
in the name of the Father,
    the Son and the Holy Spirit.
Amen!

*O God, the Awe-full One, who created heaven and earth and who has blessed humanity with so many good things, give me through your graciousness, the gift of the best faith, goodness, wisdom, and good humour, and the strength to withstand demonic forces and to drive evil away as we complete your will for each of us.*
*Earliest recorded German Christian prayer, c. 400*

**June 9**

*The 'grace-universe', in which we live and move and have our being is both concentric and anti-centrifugal: the closer you are pulled towards the Holy Hub, the nearer you come to others, and the nearer you come to others the closer you will be drawn to God.*
*Josh Doulos, pastor, Australia, born 1965*


Christ, my awesome Friend,
    please draw me deeper into your heart.
Leave no room at all
    for things second-rate,
    devious, corrupt and ugly.
In the beauty of your holiness
    may I find my purest happiness
    and my sweetest rest.
Spirit of Christ, Holy Friend,
    may I dwell within your heart.
Yes, and you in my heart
    where I may live with you forever.
Amen!


*Lord Jesus, you stretched out your arms of love on the hard wood of the cross, that all people might come within the reach of your saving embrace; Clothe us in your Spirit, that we, stretching out our hands in loving service, may bring to those who do not know you an awareness and love of you; who with the Father and the Holy Spirit live and reign, One God forever! Amen!*
*Charles Brent, Protestant Episcopal Bishop, USA, 1862-1929*

**June 10**

*In the dew of many little things the heart finds its new day and is refreshed.*

                    *Kahlil Gibran, poet, Lebanon, 1883-1931*

God of the Carpenter's home,
be with us in our home,
    enable each member of this family
    to contribute to the happiness of all,
an enable all of us
    to respect, nurture, and enhance
    the unique identity of each one,
Through Jesus Christ
    our best brother and lord.
Amen!

*I am bending my knee*
    *in the eye of the Father who created me,*
    *in the eye of the Son who purchased me,*
    *in the eye of the Spirit who cleansed me,*
    *with friendship and affection.*
*Bestow upon us fullness in our need:*
    *love towards God and the affection of God,*
    *the smile of God and the wisdom of God,*
    *the grace of God and the awe of God,*
    *and the perfect will of God;*
*through shade and light, each day and night;*
*each time in kindness, give to us your Spirit.*

                    *Ancient Gaelic prayer*

**June 11**

*She [your soul] will bring forth your true self if she lets God laugh in her and she laughs in God. There is nothing in the ground of God that cannot dance for joy.*

*Meister Eckhart, author and mystic, Germany, 1260-1328*

Loving Creator,
    let the fulsome benediction
and testimony of this homeland
    be upon our children
    and their children's children:
The blessing of wide beaches and cleansing seas,
    of forests, streams, and ferny gullies,
of sunset glory over desert plains,
    silky oaks and river gums,
and at night, the mercy of sweet sleep
    under the expansive 'glory
    of the everlasting stars'.
Amen!

*O my God, bestow upon us such confidence, such peace, and such happiness in you, that your will may be dearer to us than our own will, and your pleasure than our own pleasure. All that you give is your free gift to us, all that you take away is your grace to us. Be thanked for all, praised for all, loved for all; through Jesus Christ our Lord. Amen.*

*Christina Rossetti, poet, England, 1830-1894*

**June 12**


*In my prayers I gather around me all things God ever creates – birds beasts, fish, leaves, grass, plants, flowers; even the tiny specks of dust that gleam in the sunshine, and the little drops of dew that fall from heaven; and I urge them all to join in lifting up their hearts to God!*

*Heinrich Suso, preacher and mystic, Germany, c. 1295-1366*


If find myself in the arid bad-lands of disillusionment,
    and I'm tempted to let my faith wither,
come with the monsoon of your Holy Spirit
    and with torrential rains drench my days
until the wild flowers begin to bloom again
    in the deserts of my doubting.
Through Christ Jesus, our Spirit-filled Lord.
Amen!


*If our mouths were filled with the songs of the seas, our lips with praise as beautiful as the night skies; if our eyes shone brightly like sun and moon, and our thoughts soared up like eagles' wings; if our arms reached wide to embrace the world and our feet were as swift as the wild deer: we could not begin to thank you enough, God of abounding regeneration.*

*Adapted from a Jewish prayer*

**June 13**

*Theologians have felt no hesitation in founding a system of speculative thought on the teachings of Jesus; and yet Jesus was never an inhabitant of the realm of speculative thought.*
      *Walter Rauschenbusch, Baptist social activist, USA, 1861-1918*

Eternal God, our dwelling place,
      when the acids of modernity
      eat away at our serenity,
and combine with our private
      worries about change, decay,
      and our labyrinthine fears of death,
sound the gospel in our ears again
      and enable us to stake our life
      on your utter faithfulness.
Through Christ Jesus our Saviour.
      Amen!

*Grant, gracious Father, that I may never dispute the reasonableness of your will, but ever embrace it as the best that can happen. Prepare me always for whatever your bountiful providence brings forth. Let me not grumble, be dejected or impatient under any of the trouble of this life, but to find comfort and peace in knowing this is the will of my Father; for Jesus Christ's sake. Amen.*
      *Thomas Wilson, Bishop, Isle of Man, 1663-1755*

**June 14**

*I have no future, if you, Jesus , are not my future.*
  *Attributed to Huub Oosterhuis, theologian, poet and social activist,*
                                    *Netherlands, born 1933*


Will you, brother, Jesus,
    who are the antithesis of Mammon,
come quickly with your gospel sword
    and cut the bewitched free
    from the thraldom of possessions
    and from the tyranny of discontent
which always follows hard
    on the tinselled train of that insatiable god
    of fake hopes and vain dreams.
In your graciousness may we breathe freely again
    within that fellowship of the redeemed
    where is found the amazing contentment
    of abundant life, light and holy bliss.
Amen!


*My God, I want your guidance and direction in all I do. May your*
*wisdom counsel me, your hand lead me, and your arm support me. I*
*put myself into your hands. Breathe into me holy and heavenly*
*desires. Conform me to your own ways. Make me like my Saviour.*
*Enable me in some measure to live here on earth as He lived, and to*
*act in all things as he would have acted. Amen.*
        *Ashton Oxendon, Bishop of Montreal, Canada, 1808-1892*

**June 15**

*If we met a god who always cured us of a cold in the head, or got us into the dry train just before the rain began to team down, he would seem so absurd a god that he would have to be abolished even if he did exist.*

*Friedrich Nietzsche, philosopher, Germany, 1844-1900*

For refusing to yield
   to my anxious demands,
for forcing me to use
   my every faculty
in order finally make
   a difficult decision,
for forcing me to go it alone
   when I pleaded for a crutch:
I thank you dearly,
   God of formidable love.
Amen!

*Have mercy on those who see no further than their possessions, on all of us who have become captive to consumerism. Lord, let not the sounds of our faithlessness, the cries of our anxieties, the noise of our running to and fro, drown out the symphony of praise that rightly belongs to you.*

*Ron Gordon, UCA minister and writer, Australia, born 1932*

**June 16**

*The touching, entrancing beauty of Christianity . . . its greatness, its special genius consists, as much as in anything else, in that it is without fastidiousness.*
*Baron von Hügel, spiritual director, Austria and England,*
*1852-1925*

Slowly, loving Christ Jesus, I think I am at last starting 'to get you';
    I get your idiosyncratic values, your disreputable godliness.
    and your scary, incarnational immanence.
You are not merely in hyperbole but in very truth –
    the hungry African child desperate for food and drink,
    the boat-people waiting to be welcomed to a new beginning,
    the lone prisoner in the security block needing a friendly visit,
    the ill, yet prickly, neighbour who craves a helping hand,
    the street kids urgent for some warm clothing.
Lord Jesus, I think I am beginning 'to get you'.
    but am I ready to truly meet and succour you?
Lord have mercy, Christ have mercy.
    Lord have mercy, on me a sinner.
Amen!

*Grant, Lord, grant us the grace to desire you with our complete affections, so that desiring you we may find you, and finding you may love you; and in loving you may hate those sins which cut us off from you; for the sake of Jesus Christ. Amen.*
*St. Anselm, Archbishop of Canterbury, England, 1033-1109*

**June 17**


*And I know that the hand of God is the promise of my own,*
*And I know that the spirit of God is the brother of my own*
*And that all men ever born are also my brothers*
*And the women my sisters and lovers*
*And that the kelson [keel-board] of the creation is love.*
*Walt Whitman, poet, USA, 1819-1892*


Incognito Christ,
    our true brother Jesus,
you come when we least expect you
    at times not of our choosing
    and in people not always to our liking.
Please do not be put off
    by our slowness
in accepting your rebuke
    from an opponent or rival,
or by our reluctance
    to answer your cry for help
from a stranger in dire straits.
    For your loves' sake;
Amen!


*Lord Jesus, the house of my soul is narrow; I want to enlarge it, that*
*you may enter in. It is in ruins, please repair it. To what carpenter*
*can I call for help, to clear and repair it, but you? Cleanse me from*
*my secret faults, O Lord, and spare your servant. Amen!*
*Adapted from St. Augustine, Bishop of Hippo, North Africa,*
*354-430*

**June 18**

*Whoever sets any bounds for the reconstructive power of the religious life over the social relations and institutions of men, to that extent denies the faith of the Master.*
*Walter Rauschenbusch, Baptist social activist, USA, 1861-1918*

At times, God, our political scene is so complex
and confusing that we don't know how to pray.
Experience has slowly taught us
that some Christian politicians make poor leaders,
while some others who claim to be of scant faith
are surprisingly dedicated to the common good.
You alone, God, can see the way our nation should go
and who will make the best leaders.
Whenever we come to cast our vote,
not our will, but yours be done.
Amen!

*Keep us, O Lord, from the vain strife of many words, and grant us a constant profession of faith. Preserve us in the way of enlighten-ment, so that we may hold fast to those vows professed when we were baptised into the name of the Father, and of the Son, and of the Holy Ghost, and that we may glorify you, our Creator, Redeemer and Sanctifier. Amen .*
*Hilary, Bishop of Poitiers, France, c. 315-367*

**June 19**

*Rule 2: Two afternoons a week should be given to working with the poor. Drop introspection and turn to thoughts and acts for others.*
*Evelyn Underhill, author and mystic, England, 1875-1941*

Incomparable Christ, the Joy of loving hearts,
    whenever we meet together for worship,
    fellowship or community service,
    reprogram us with your attitude.
Give us the capacity to work boldly and humbly
    with the risks and opportunities which confront us,
    knowing that nothing is ahead of your foresight
    nor outside of your providence.
Through your wonder-full name.
    Amen!

*O God, you made me for yourself, to show forth your goodness through me. Show forth, I humbly pray, the life-giving power of your nature, help me to such a true and lively faith, such a thirst after the life and spirit of your Son, Jesus, in my soul that all that is within me may be turned from every inward thought to outward action in your service. Amen.*
*William Law, Puritan writer, England, 1686-1761*

**June 20**

*May God animate us with cheerfulness, fortify us against disappointment and calamity, emancipate us from dejection, and give us a joyful sense of our daily blessings.*

*Author unknown*

Blessed are the songs of birds at dawn,
    blessed the laughter of little children,
    blessed the prayers of saints and martyrs,
but ever most blessed,
    ever most beautiful,
    ever most adorable,
is the ineffable, awesome delight
    of your Divine Stillness,
O God of endless wonders,
    the Soul-Peace of the universe!
Amen!

*I lie down this night with God, and God will lie down with me.*
*I lie down this night with Christ, and Christ will lie down with me.*
*I lie down this night with Spirit, and Spirit will lie down with me.*
*God and Christ and Spirit, are lying down with me this night.*

*Traditional Celtic prayer*

**June 21**

*The conquest of the earth, which mostly means the taking it away from those who have a different complexion or slightly flatter noses than ourselves, is not a pretty thing when you look into it too much.*
*Joseph Conrad, Polish-English author, England, 1857-1924*

God of the least and lowliest,
    we pray for the little nations of the world.
In the assemblies of the United Nations,
    raise up prophets who will plead their cause.
In all their diplomatic activity,
    give them the integrity and wisdom
to withstand bribery or bullying
    from powerful nations.
Speed the day when the small will be honoured
    and heard as much as the superpowers.
For the sake of the world for whom Christ Jesus
    gave his all.
Amen!

*Take from us, O Lord, all pride and vanity, all boasting and self-assertion. Give us the true courage that shows itself in gentleness, the true wisdom that shows itself in simplicity; and the true power that shows itself in modesty. Through Jesus Christ our Lord. Amen.*
*Charles Kingsley, minister and social reformer, England,*
*1819-1875*

**June 22**

*Remove from the Christian religion its ability to shock and Christianity is altogether destroyed. It then becomes a tiny and, superficial thing capable of neither inflicting deep wounds or of healing them.*

*Soren Kierkegaard, philosopher, Denmark, 1813-1855*

Disturber Spirit,
    the disrupter of false peace,
the rushing Wind
    that breaks as well as bends,
the flowing Water
    that floods as well as cleanses,
the tongue of Fire
    that welds as well as warms:
Please do not let up on your people
    or give us over to our own devices.
Persist with your fiercest mercy
    and forge us, Jesus-like.
Amen!

*Holy Spirit, my dearest Sister and Companion, grant that I may never settle for the lesser when the greater, by your grace, is possible, nor allow me to pursue ambitions, no matter how noble, that you have not chosen for me. Disrupt and discomfort any of your projects that are not for me to undertake; support and comfort me in those difficult ministries that you have, in fact, laid at my door. Amen!*

*Magda Christopher, feminist author, Australia, born 1987*

**June 23**

*The pale waning moon fades slowly in the dawn*
*and a temple bell calls across the frosted lawn.*
                    *Anonymous poet, Ch'ing dynasty, China, c. 1644*

Spirit of the morning star,
    I bless you for the day that is dawning,
Spirit of dear mother earth,
    I bless you for gifts unfolding,
Spirit of the multitude of living things,
    I bless you for the calls and songs abounding,
Spirit of my human sisters and brothers,
    I bless you for the potential which is awaking,
Spirit of the eternal Man of Nazareth,
    I bless you for all flowering and fruiting,
Spirit of the One God, source and sustenance of
    all that is or ever will be,
all honour and glory are yours this day.
Amen!

*Make us, loving Lord, to flourish like white lilies in your courts, and*
*to shed around on other believers the fragrance of good works, and*
*the example of a faithful life; through your mercy and love. Amen.*
                    *Spanish prayer, c. 6th-11th century*

**June 24**

*And all must love the human form,*
*in heathen Turk and Jew,*
*Where Mercy, Love and Pity dwell,*
*there God is dwelling too.*
                    *William Blake, poet and artist, England, 1757-1827*

Thank you, Lord Jesus,
    for the way you confront us
    and turn upside down
    our shallow ideas and values;
with you we are bold to say:
    go well, pure of heart;
    go well, poor in Spirit;
    go well, merciful ones;
    go well, peacemakers;
    go well, meek of the earth,
to you belongs the new age of God!
Amen!

*O Lord Jesus Christ, give such a good measure of your Spirit that we*
*may control anger, act mercifully, moderate our desires, increase*
*our loving, shake off gloom, cast away pride, never become*
*vindictive, and not fear death; ever trusting our lives to you, the one*
*immortal God. Amen.*
                    *Apollonius, Christian martyr, Asia Minor, c. 15 – c. 100*

**June 25**

*Never throw away any person. People need to be restored, renewed, revived, reclaimed, and redeemed.*
        *Attributed to Audrey Hepburn, actress, England 1929-1993*

Open the shutters within our minds,
    that your light may flood in.
Open up the doors of our hearts,
    that your love may occupy us.
Open up the cupboards of our spirits,
    that you may clean out stagnation.
O God of Jesus and our God,
    make us more yours today than yesterday
and when tomorrow arrives pristine,
    make us open for more of your love
and ready to take delight in common things.
    Through Jesus, the true Son of Man
    who is the fountain of holy abundance.
    Amen!

*Remember, O Lord, of what I am made, that I am but human. Take pity on my weakness, and support my frail nature. You know the temptations I suffer, how they surge within me, and the storm they raise. You know me through and through. Lord have mercy. Amen.*
        *St. Isidore, Archbishop of Seville, Spain, c. 560-636*

**June 26**

*No, matter how distant I might feel from the mystery of God, that man Jesus will not let me go. Nothing else in life makes such deep sense to me.*

*Robert Renton, UCA minister and educationalist, Australia,*
*born 1946*

Christ Jesus,
    the Heart of my hoping
    and the Soul of my seeking,
    hear this is my morning prayer:
Redeem me from a plump yet shallow belief
    to a slimmer and much deeper faith;
and then, when I my roots search far down
    into the Ground and Joy of my belonging,
please guide me to choose between
    what are the next practical loving deeds
that you are calling me to tackle first,
    and to know and which are the ones
    that will be better left to someone else,
    known or unknown to me,
at your good time and of your wise choosing.
    For your love's sake.
Amen!

*O Lord, give us more charity, more self-denial, more likeness to you. Teach us to sacrifice our comforts to others, and our likings for the sake of doing good.*

*Thomas à Kempis, scholar, Germany, 1380-1471*

**June 27**

*I hope we shall crush in their birth those moneyed corporations which dare already to challenge our government to a trial by strength, and bid defiance to the laws of our country.*
        Thomas Jefferson, third President of the USA, 1743-1826

Jesus, you turned your ears
    to the blind.
You rested your eyes
    on the deaf,
You stretched your hands
    to the leper,
And in the awful hour
    of inexorable love,
you gave your body
    for us all:
O Lamb of God,
    you take away
the ills of the world,
    amazing is your Name!
Amen!

*Eternal God, lay to rest the resistance of our passion, indolence or fear; consecrate with your presence the way our feet may go; that the humblest work will shine, and the roughest places be made plain. Lift us above unrighteous anger and mistrust into faith and hope and charity by a simple and steadfast reliance on your will; in all things draw us to the mind of Christ,*
        James Martineau, Unitarian scholar, France, 1805-1900

**June 28**

*When y're, like confused, don't rush mad around in circle; you know, like a frightened bandicoot? Bi still, and wait. When y're stiller, stand up, and bi brave t'do best y'cn' do.*
> *Attributed to an Indigenous farm hand, Colac region, Australia,*
> *date unknown*

O Lord, only you know what is best for me.
Let this or that be done as you please.
  Give whatever you will,
  how much you will
  and whenever you will.
For your Name's sake,
Amen!

*Jesus Christ, sometimes my need and exhaustion seem great and you seem very silent. Stony and hard conditions surround me. Yet those are the moments when my faith is purified, when I am given my chance of gaining patience and fortitude and tranquillity.*
> *Evelyn Underhill, author and mystic, England, 1875-1941*

**June 29**

*I, your God, am there for all beings; my love never varies. But for those who love me, I am in them and they are in me.*
*Bhagavad Gita, Hindu Scriptures, India, c. 600 BC*

A thousand thanks, O God,
   and a thousand more,
   for your true Son, our Brother.
He lived our common life
   with a flair which has left
   the centuries gasping.
He embraced our death
   with an awe-filled,
   trembling passion
which has opened
   the doors of limitless life.
   to all humanity.
Blessed is this humble One
   who comes in your name!
   Glory in the Highest!
Amen!

*O blessed Jesus Christ, you bid all who carry heavy burdens to come to you; please refresh us with your presence and power. Quieten our thoughts and give ease to our hearts, by bringing us closer to those things which are eternal. Amen.*
*Evelyn Underhill, author and mystic, England, 1875-1941*

**June 30**

*God,*
*unleash from the inside*
*your wild and trusting child*
*hands held*
*high for swinging*
*laughter let loose and ringing*
            *Jennie Gordon, UCA minister and poet, Australia, born 1962*

Precious the fingers that anointed blind eyes,
     the hands that touched lepers,
     the arms that embraced little ones.
Precious the smile that welcomed outcasts,
     the frown that rebuked the arrogant
     the tongue that told parables.
Precious the courage that led to Jerusalem.
     the faith that agonised in Gethsemane,
     the love that suffered at Golgotha.
Precious the lips that gave the Easter greeting,
     the mercy which restored ashamed disciples,
     the spirit let loose in the whole world.
Blessed is the Christ who comes
     in the name of the Lord God!
Amen!

*Lord, I desire that at all times, those who benefit by my daily work*
*may not only be refreshed in body, but may also be drawn closer to*
*your love and refreshed in all your goodness.*
            *St. Gertrude, Cistercian nun, Germany, 1256-1302*

**July 1**

*I have done with barren strife and dark imaginings*
*and in my future work and life will seek the better things.*

Henry Lawson, poet, Australia, 1867-1922

God, our beginning and our end,
    help us to turn your way that our faces
    may begin to reflect your glory.
Use even the accidental, hurtful,
    caustic and abrasive experiences
    to polish us into mirrors,
so that other people may catch in us
    a glimpse of the loveliness
    of your light, love, and laughter.
Through the Son who is the very aurora
    of your love, truth, and joy.
    Amen!

*You, O Lord, have called us to watch and pray. Therefore, whatever*
*may be the sin in others against which we protest, make us careful*
*to watch against that same sin in ourselves. In order to perform this*
*duty aright, grant us grace to preserve a sober, equal temper, and*
*sincerity to pray for your assistance. Amen.*
*  Susannah Wesley, scholar and educationalist, England, 1669-1742*

**July 2**

*God is not an individual. He is the absolute personality, in whom all other persons have their ground, yet who is more than all.*
*P.T. Forsyth, theologian, England, 1848-1921*

Divine Friend,
    go with each member of our family,
that they may travel safely,
    work gladly, laugh kindly,
and at the end of the day
    return home cheerfully.
Through Christ our Saviour.
Amen!

*Eternal God, you are both host and guest. You invite us to your table of life, and come and share with us in your love. Your open table is wider than the earth and your food is everlasting. Continue to be our guest, Lord Jesus, that we may find new life and become aware of the needs of the world around us; we ask in your name. Amen.*
*Ron Gordon, UCA minister and writer, Australia, born 1932*

**July 3**


*The best adventures are not outside a person but within them.*
*Mary Anne Evans (pen name George Eliot) novelist and journalist,*
*England, 1819-1880*


We praise you for every reminder
    that your best name is love,
At morning or evening, you are love,
    in sunlight or shadow, you are love,
in youth or age, health or weakness,
    in life or death, your name is love.
Blessed be your best and dearest name,
    on our lips and in our deeds,
today and forever.
    Amen!


*O Lord, who hast mercy upon all, take away from me my sins and*
*mercifully rekindle in me the fire of your Holy Spirit. Soften within*
*me this heart of stone, and make it a heart of flesh and blood, a*
*heart able to love and adore You, a heart to delight in You and be*
*passionate to follow and to enjoy You; for Christ's sake. Amen!*
*St. Ambrose, Bishop of Milan, Italy, c. 339-397*

**July 4**

*All endeavour calls for the ability to tramp the last mile, shape the last objective, endure the last hour's toil. The fight to the finish spirit is the one characteristic we must possess if we are to face the future as finishers.*
                    Henry David Thoreau, philosopher, USA, 1817-1862

All-wise and loving God,
 hear our prayers for our homeland.
We know that the collective wisdom
 of political leaders is sadly inadequate,
and the vision behind even the best legislation
 can get lost in bureaucratic administration.
Therefore send upon our leaders
 your Spirit of larger wisdom,
and upon the thousands of our civil servants
 a spirit of humble, clear-sightedness,
that more of your just and compassionate ways may
 be known and practiced in this nation.
To your honour and praise alone;
 though Christ Jesus our Lord.
Amen!

*O God, grant us a new vision for our nation, as fair as she might be: a people of justice, where none shall prey on others; a people of plenty, where vice and poverty shall not fester; a people of brotherhood, where success shall be founded on service; a people of peace, where order shall not rest on force but on love for all. Hear the prayer of all our hearts as we each pledge our time, strength and thought to speed your final coming day of beauty and righteousness. Amen!*
                    *Walter Rauschenbusch, Baptist social activist, USA, 1861-1918*

**July 5**

*I think it is an insult to God to make the same requests each day. It is as much to say, he is deaf, or very slow of comprehension.*
        *Evelyn Underhill (when aged 17), author and mystic, England,*
                                                                *1875-1941*

Generous God,
    forgive the way we ration our outreach,
    and the poverty of our prayers.
Give to us, we earnestly pray,
    the disciplined, priceless liberality
    of the man of Nazareth,
that in both our praying and serving
    his generosity may fashion our life-style.
For his love's sake.
Amen!

*O Lord, the author and persuader of peace, love and goodwill, soften our hard, steely hearts, that we may wish well on one another, as true disciples of Jesus Christ. Give us the graciousness to show forth the heavenly life, wherein there is neither disagreement nor hatred, but peace and love on all hands, one towards another. Through Jesus Christ. Amen.*
                                                        *Author unknown*

**July 6**

*The poorest ploughman is in Christ equal with the greatest prince that ever lived.*

*William Tyndale, Bible translator, England, c. 1492-1536*

This day, Friend of the humble and poor,
    we pray for those who are suffering
    the ache and anxiety of loneliness.
Forget neither the need of
    the migrant, the child, the aged,
    nor the deserted wife or abused husband,
neither the homeless teenage runaway,
    nor the new arrival to a strange city,
    or the shy person alone in a flat
Spirit of the truest friendship,
    thaw in them the ice of loneliness
    and give them the warmth and peace
of your blessed companionship.
    Amen!

*Lord Jesus, many of us are waiting for you:*
*the war-torn are waiting for peace,*
*the hungry are waiting for bread.*
*the refugees are waiting for a homeland,*
*the sick are waiting for healers.*
*Have you forgotten us? O Lord,*
*come quickly, we pray. Amen.*

*Attributed to a woman of the Congo, date unknown*

**July 7**


*When you arise in the morning, give thanks for the food and for the joy of living. If you see no reason for giving thanks, the fault lies only in yourself.*
>        *Attributed to Chief Tecumseh, Native American, Shawnee Nation,*
>                                                                    *USA, 1768-1813*


When the landscape seems barren
    and our thirst is considerable,
we thank you, loving one,
    that there is always beneath us
abundant artesian refreshment
    for those who are faithful
and willing to dig deep
and find out for themselves.
Amen!


*Soften our hearts, O Lord, that we may be moved no less at the troubles and sorrows of our neighbours as if they were our dearest friends, or even ourselves. So we may be stirred with compassion and undertake whatever measures we can to alleviate their hungers, sorrows or other discomforts.*
*Amen.*
>             *Johannes Ludovicus Vives, humanist scholar, Spain and*
>                                         *the Netherlands, 1492-1540*

**July 8**

*Ambitious people climb, but faithful people build.*
*Julia Ward Howe, poet and abolitionist, USA, 1819-1910*

Holy Friend keep me sincere, simple,
    and disingenuous in all I do for you.
Should I act swiftly on a good and loving impulse,
    let it be governed and blessed by you.
Whenever I take considerable risks in your name,
    may I blithely think is a mere, reasonable service.
And should I exceed my own expectations,
    let me bask in a satisfaction purged of hubris.
For your love's sake.
    Amen!

*I ask You, O God – and whatever other gods may haunt this world –*
*to give me beauty in my soul, and may the outer and inner 'me' be*
*as one. May I have only as much gold as a temperate man can carry*
*in his wallet. This prayer, I think, is enough for me just now.*
*Attributed to Socrates, Athenian philosopher, Greece, 469-399 BC*

**July 9**


*If you want to become a church leader, what you must learn to wield is not a critic's pen or a judge's gavel but a feet-washer's towel.*
*Magda Christopher, feminist author, Australia, born 1987*


Loving God,
    whenever I discover myself in a church committee
where egos are jousting for supremacy,
    enable me to be smart and keep my cool.
Give me your sensible and generous Spirit
    that I may disarm them with a smile,
neutralise them with an intuitive word,
    and assist them to regain their bearings
in seeking to know and accomplish your will.
    In the name of Jesus,
whose strength was grace and whose ego was all love.
    Amen!


*Bless us, O God, with the love of you and of our neighbours. Give us a serene conscience, the command of our feelings, and for the remainder, your will be done! O prince of peace, keep us in your love and charity. Amen.*
*Thomas Wilson, Bishop, Isle of Man, 1663-1755*

**July 10**

*God has chosen not to do without us any more than we can do without him.*
> *Meister Eckhart, author and mystic, Germany, 1260-1328*

Nurture within us, God of surprises,
    your gift of resilient faith
which can transform setbacks into growth,
    suffering into deepening wisdom,
    sorrow into healing tears,
and by the alchemy of your saving grace
    can transfigure despair into holy optimism.
Through Christ Jesus, our Redeemer.
Amen!

*Lord, who on earth can adequately sing your praises? What can my eye see with which I can liken you? What music is there with which to compare you? You are above me, below me, within me and without. All exist in you, all are from you, you give us everything, you withhold nothing. Who on earth can worthily sing your praises?*
> *From an Egyptian inscription, c. 4 BC*

**July 11**

*We should never meet a human need without attempting to do something about it.*
> *St. Mary MacKillop, social activist, Australia, 1842-1909*

The trouble with your true saints, God,
    is that they largely practice what they preach!
That can leave the rest of us stragglers
    with a lot of 'egg on our faces'.
Please, do not permit us to bog down in self-pity;
    make us willing to accept forgiveness
for our falling short of good practice
    and to return with renewed vigour
to the tasks "your wisdom has assigned".
    In spirit of Christ and to his praise and glory.
Amen!

*O God, help us to 'get over ourselves' that we may give over our lives to you, with our particular gifts and skills, and with all that we are and possess. Through Christ Jesus our Lord. Amen!*
> *Jacob Boehme, shoemaker and mystic, Germany, 1575-1624*

**July 12**

*It is better to heed the rebuke of the wise, than to listen to the popular songs of fools.*

> *Attributed to Qoheleth, 'The Preacher', Ecclesiastes,*
> *date unknown*

You, loving God,
are the giver of time and opportunity;
    help us on those flat, hangover days
    which follow on lively, exciting yesterdays.
Keep us civil with those around us,
    and assist us to focus on small duties
    as we would on mighty matters.
Keep us alert to your small blessings
    and if we fail to recognise many of them,
then during today make us a blessing
    to some other pilgrim soul.
For your love's sake.
Amen!

*O God, you are worthy of an infinite love, I have nothing which can adequately measure your dignity but such is my desire toward you, that if I had all that you have, I would gladly resign it all to you. Amen.*

> *Gertrude More, Benedictine nun, England, 1606-1633*

**July 13**

*I have lived long enough to be able to thank God that all my prayers
have not been answered.*

*Jean Ingelow, poet, England, 1820-1897*

For refusing to yield
    to my anxiety-driven prayers,
for forcing me to put to use
    my full rational faculty,
and for leaving me to go it alone
    when I pleaded for a crutch:
I thank you, God of hard refusals.
    Through Christ Jesus,
my most patient Redeemer.
Amen!

*How can anything, O God, separate us from your love? As the lotus
lily belongs to the water, so do we belong to you; as the albatross
rides the winds, so do we soar with you. From the very beginning
until beyond the ending, there will always be your love bringing us
together!*

*Author unknown – maybe Kabir, mystic and poet, India,
c. 1440 – c. 1518*

**July 14**

*open our lives*
*to your lifted hands of blessing*
*release the songs of joy*
*birthed in this ruptured time*
*and let your house*
*be ours and mine.*
                    *Jennie Gordon, UCA minister and poet, Australia, born 1962*


God of hope, the world's sure salvation,
     in this savage and disfigured world
     we yearn for the golden age of peace.
Enable your people of faith and hope
     to go on paying the price of love,
     that peacemaking may expand
into every parcel of the globe
     and all people become the recipients
of a love that is much more,
     but never less, than basic justice.
Through the costly grace of Christ;
Amen!


*Father, pardon our past gratitude and disobedience; and purify us,*
*whether by your gentler or your sterner dealings, till we have done*
*your will on earth and your remove us to your nearer presence with*
*the redeemed in heaven. Amen.*
                    *Mary Carpenter, social reformer, England, 1807-1887*

**July 15**

*A man may be a tough, concentrated, successful money-maker and
never contribute to his country anything more than a horrible example.*
*Attributed to Robert Menzies, the longest serving Prime Minister,
Australia, 1894-1978*

God of deserts and all wilderness places,
    there are times when this bustling city
    seems to be an harsh urban wilderness
where the hungry of spirit go empty
    and the meek die alone, thirsting for a sip of grace.
Please lead your needy ones to those unexpected places
    among these barren city canyons
where we can still receive without money
    your nourishing, heavenly manna,
and those rocky events from which can freely flow
    your life regenerating waters.
Amen!

*O my Lord, what a great comfort it is that you did not entrust the
fulfilment of your will to one so useless as I am! I thank you forever!
Let all things praise you! As things stand, Lord, though my will is not
yet free from self-interest, I freely hand it over to you.*
*St. Teresa of Avila, nun and mystic, Spain, 1515-1582*

**July 16**

*Nothing great is ever achieved without much enduring.*
          St. Catherine of Siena, Dominican mystic, Italy, 1347-1380

As we close the cover
     on this long, working day,
loving God, let your benediction
     rest on those dear people
     who are so precious to us
     yet infinitely more dear to you,
Grant to them this evening
     forgiveness for their errors,
     gratitude for their blessings,
     a quiet night's sleep,
     and hope for tomorrow.
Through Christ Jesus our Master.
     Amen!

*Grant me, I beg you, my God, in the name of Jesus Christ your Son,
the charity which never fails, that my light may shine, warming my
own heart and enlightening the path of others. Amen.*
          St. Columbanus, Irish missionary, France, 543-615

**July 17**

*May your people add light to the lives that have become confusion,*
*and add hope where folk have lapsed into hopelessness.*
                    *Ron Gordon, UCA minister and writer, Australia, born 1932*


O generous Source of time and space,
the loving Saviour of fools and rebels,
and joyful Counsellor to the children of earth,
    yours is the kingdom of hope-fullness,
    the power of saving grace-fullness
    and the endless glory of crucified loveliness,
forever and ever!
    Amen!


*Bountiful Creator, we praise and thank you for the wonders of this*
*remarkable world. What is more wonderful, you place us here with*
*your spirit-breath within us; your miracle, we are a world within a*
*world. We emerge from nowhere to exercise reason, faith and love*
*within this paradise of delight. To you our praise, to you our hymns,*
*to you all honour and glory, for ever and ever! Amen!*
                    *Apostolic Constitutions, Syria, c. 375-380*

**July 18**

*Every generation tries to put its doctrine on a high shelf where the children cannot reach it.*
        *Walter Rauschenbusch, Baptist social activist, USA, 1861-1918*

Spirit of all seasons,
        during the sour winters
        of my soul's discontent
                please prepare the deep ground
                        of my being for the seeds
                        of your choosing.
        May I be ready and waiting
        for the sprouting and flowering
        of whatever new springtime
with which you decide to bless me.
                        For your love's sake,
Amen!

*God, you have folded back the mantle of the night, to clothe us in the golden glory of the day, chase from our hearts all gloomy thoughts, and make us glad with the brightness of hope, that we may effectively aspire to unwon virtues; through Jesus Christ our Lord. Amen.*
                        *Ancient collect, origin uncertain*

**July 19**

*Dreams only become holy when they are put into action.*
*Adelaide E. Procter, poet, England, 1825-1864*

Holy God, we confess to each other and to you that we have been
unworthy stewards in your creation:
> We have plundered the earth and exploited it without due care
> for its diverse plants, creatures and beauty, with scant love for
> future generations.

We confess to each other and to you that we have been grossly
deficient carers of one another:
> We have lavished attention on a few, a despised many,
> over-valued our own importance and down-valued others,
> and despoiled life with our arrogance.

God of astounding forbearance, we do repent:
> Let us start again as stewards with a high calling, as carers with
> an often costly love to share, and as believers who really do
> practice their faith.

Through Christ Jesus our hope and our joy.
Amen!

*O God, deliver us from all ugly earthly desires, that no sin may reign*
*in us, but that we may, with free spirits, love and serve you.*
*Through Jesus Christ. Amen.*
*Gelasian Prayers, France, c. 6th-7th century*

**July 20**

*Precious was the inheritance of the Jews, but now it has been superseded because the inheritance of Christ's grace is poured out on all people.*

*Melito, Bishop of Sardis, died c. 180*

Loving God and holy Friend
we pray for self-understanding,
    that we may sincerely repent,
for simple, genuine faith
    that we may trust your mercy;
and for constancy in loving,
    that we may ever adore
    the Source of our salvation.
Amen!

*Everything belongs to you, Good of beauty,*
*Everything belongs to you, God of wisdom,*
*Everything belongs to you, God of justice,*
*Everything belongs to you, God of endless mercies.*
*To you be glory now and forever. Amen.*

*Clement of Alexandria, theologian, c. 150 – c. 215*

**July 21**

*Better to have few possessions and the love of God, than to have immense wealth with anxiety.*
> Attributed to King Solomon, Jerusalem, c. 950 BC

Loving Spirit of long range goals
    and immediate mercies,
set me free from faithless worry
    and from petulant frustration;
Save me, not only from jumping at shadows
    and tilting at windmills,
but also rescue me from fretting about matters
    that lie beyond my reach.
 So ground me in your providence
    and sweeten me with your grace
that I may cheerfully do whatever I can
    and leave the rest to other believers.
To your praise and glory;
Amen!

*O God, worthy of an infinite love, I have nothing with which to adequately applaud your dignity; but such is my yearning honour you that if I possessed all that you have; I would gladly resign all to you.*
> Gertrude More, Benedictine nun, England, 1606-1633

**July 22**

*If a poor man or woman comes into your church, whether they are known or strangers, and especially if they are frail or elderly, and there should be no chair for them, the bishop himself should make room for them, even if he has to sit on the floor.*
                          *An unknown bishop, Northern Syria, 3rd century*

Merciful God,
in this era of economic rationalism
     when greed and opulence
     are lauded as the 'good life',
it is hard for us to keep our eyes fixed
     and our daily activities focussed
     on the positive poverty of Christ.
Please continue to be an irritant within;
     do not permit us become complacent
     and get sucked in by the lure of Mammon.
Do not allow us settle for anything less
     than the gospel of Christ Jesus
     and the values of your kingdom.
Amen!

*Holy God, we see the possibility your rule in human affairs, in the life, words and deeds of Jesus who confirms for us that life can be full and rich and free without the lust for power and the rewards of wealth.*
                    *Ron Gordon, UCA minister and writer, Australia, born 1932*

**July 23**

*Most people are bothered by those passages of Scripture they do not understand, but the passages that bother me are those I do understand.*

Mark Twain, author, USA, 1835-1910

Most holy Friend,
    whenever we try to evade you
    by busying ourselves
    with the difficulties of faith,
stop us in our tracks.

Confront us with those truths
    which we understand all too well
    yet do not yet live by;
    for your mercy's shake,
Amen!

*Helpers of the helpless, saviour of the lost, home of the wanderer, health of the sick, please remember for good those that love us, those that hate us, and those we have forgotten. You know each person's need, and hear each prayer, please grant to each according to your loving kindness; through Jesus Christ our Lord. Amen.*

Eastern Orthodox prayer

**July 24**

*Others look at a truly generous soul without comprehension; they don't realise how much of God's grace and help await ordinary folk who answer his call.*
*Book of Wisdom, Alexandria, Egypt, c. 100-40 BC*

We are most grateful, God our true love,
    that humanity is your pet project;
that our brokenness is mended
    by your awesome gentleness,
our foolish moves are countered
    by your long-sighted strategies,
our wounds are dressed
    by your warm, firm fingers,
and in our dark wanderings
    you pastor-soul seeks and finds us.
We are most grateful
    that we are your pet project
which shall not ultimately fail.
    Amen!

*Good God, you invite us to trust you. You ask that we are open to visions and dreams and possibilities of what our lives may yet be, that together we might grow towards you as plants grow towards the sun. Amen.*
*Ron Gordon, UCA minister and writer, Australia, born 1932*

**July 25**

*Belief consists in accepting the native affirmations of the soul;*
*unbelief, in denying them.*
    *Mary Anne Evans (pen name George Eliot) novelist and journalist,*
                                        *England, 1819-1880*

You are
    the Silence where the truth is spoken,
    the Void which is full and overflowing,
    the Turbulence where there is supreme calm,
    and the Depth which soars higher than the heavens.
You are
    the Nameless which names and weighs each sparrow,
    the Enigma who numbers the hair on our head
    the Forsakenness where the lost at last come home,
You are
    my love, my peace, my light my joy.
Hallelujah!

*O great Spirit, help me always to speak the truth gently, to listen*
*with an open mind when others are speaking, and to remember*
*that greater peace that can only be found in deepest silence.*
        *Attributed to a Native American prayer, USA, date unknown*

**July 26**

*Jesus was not regarded as a good, respectable, successful citizen; until we understand this, Christians are hiding in a religious delusion.*
*Josh Doulos, pastor, Australia, born 1965*

Jesus, Joy of loving hearts,
    blessed are you forever!
Your generosity, our meanness;
    your meekness, our arrogance;
your wisdom our foolishness;
    your eternity, our mortality;
your loveliness our tattiness;
    your love, our adoration.
O saviour and delight of the universe,
    blessed are you forever!
Amen!

*Uncreated and unequalled God, font of all loveliness, you have let loose among all races the sweet fragrance of the Gospel; bless all who are baptised that this fragrant oil may abide in them and be shed abroad. Through Jesus Christ our Lord, Amen.*
*Apostolic Constitutions, Syria, c. 375-380*

**July 27**

*We need wisdom for an attuning to new things that are happening;
as on a lyre one can play the same notes but change the rhythm, so
is the Logos changing everything.*
*Book of Wisdom, Alexandria, Egypt, c. 100-40 BC*

Lord Jesus,
help us to be pure-of-heart disciples
    drawn and shaped by a loving integrity,
sharing your values and doing your will
    as we gladly serve others
with the high spirits and deep love
    of those who are now joint heirs
with the Light of the world.
    and the very Joy of the universe!
Amen!

*Please anoint me, O God, with a friendly spirit, untiring patience, a
warm and loving heart; a kindly face, cordial speech and respect for
others; that in the intercourse of daily life, I may not unnecessarily
offend another, but as far as possible live in harmony with my
neighbours. Amen.*
*Johann Arndt, theologian and mystic, Germany, 1555-1621*

**July 28**

*when the meter*
*is lost*
*and the ransom price*
*outweighs the cost*
*love is*
*all there is.*
                    *Jennie Gordon, UCA minister and poet, Australia, born 1962*

God, you are always compassionate;
    we confess that we just 'turn off'
when chronic attention-seekers
    badger us for attention.
Give us the will and the grace to work out
    creative ways of responding to them;
ways which are not mere sops to their begging,
    or a cruel neglect of their actual needs.
For your Love's sake.
    Amen!

*Loving God, you have given us a mind to know you, a will to serve*
*you, and a soul to love you. Be with us today in all we do, so that*
*your light may shine in and through us. May we today become what*
*you have created us to be, and in all we do glorify your name.*
*Amen.*
        *Thomas More, scholar and statesman, England, 1478-1535*

**July 29**


*How can I find myself, how can I have a successful life? Without the Lord's aid, I must fail, for he alone holds my destiny in his hands.*
*Michelangelo, painter-sculptor, Italy, 1475-1564*


Most generous and patient God, have pity on us all
    for the miserly way we limit our times of worship,
and forgive the way we hoard or ration out
    our compassion for neighbours.
Give us, we pray, the disciplined liberality
    of the Man of Nazareth,
that in both our prayer and service
    his generous soul may shape our ways
    and liven up our days.
To your glory, Holy Friend;
    Amen!


*O God, you have chosen to make us your playmates. Please lead the child within each of us in your wonderful ways. May we love mercy, doing it steadfastly, and so become like you in your compassionate deeds. Fuse us into one harmony you in us and we in you, until we could not be closer, and remain so unwearied forever. Amen.*
*Mechthild of Magdeburg, mystic and social activist, Germany,*
*c. 1207 – c. 1282*

**July 30**

*Courage sisters, courage; put your trust in God who helps you in all things.*
                St. Mary MacKillop, social activist, Australia, 1842-1909


There are times, strong Master Jesus,
    when discipleship is exhausting;
like clambering along a cliff face
    where toeholds are small
and where one's fingers and arms
    cling on defiantly to the hard rock.
At such times, grant us, please, Lord,
    safe ledges for respite and rest,
and the decisive faith
    that gets moving again,
following your intrepid lead.
Amen!


*Lord Jesus Christ, no matter where we are, far away or near at hand, involved in the hurly-burly of the world, or immersed in our own cares or joys, light-hearted or down in the dumps, draw us to yourself; draw us so to yourself that we become totally yours. Amen.*
                Soren Kierkegaard, philosopher, Denmark, 1813-1855

**July 31**

*Jesus, open my heart again before you open my ears and mouth.*
*Jennie Gordon, UCA minister and poet, Australia, born 1962*


Loving God,
    as the optimism of youth recedes
    under the hard grit of daily life,
    please maintain within us
    the buoyancy of your sisterly Spirit,
    and the will-fullness of your lovely Christ.
Amen!


*I thank you, God, that I have lived*
*in this great world and known its many joys:*
*The song of birds, the strong, sweet scent of hay*
*and cooling breezes in the secret dusk,*
*the flaming sunsets at the close of day;*
*music at night, and moonlight on the sea,*
*and wild, white spray, flung high in ecstasy;*
*The faithful eyes of dogs, and treasured books,*
*the love of kin and fellowship of friends,*
*and all that makes life dear and beautiful.*
*I thank you, too, that there has come to me*
*a little sorrow and, sometimes defeat.*
*Dawn breaking after dreary hours of pain,*
*as morning light breaks through to me again.*
*Because of these and other blessings poured*
*unasked upon my wondering head,*
*because I know there is yet to come*
*an even richer and more glorious life,*
*and most of all because your only Son*
*once sacrificed life's loveliness for me –*
*I thank you, God, that I have lived.*
    *Elizabeth, Countess of Craven, England, 1750-1828*

**August 1**

*Don't say "I have found the truth" but rather "I have found some truth". For the truth unfolds itself, like a lotus flower of countless petals.*

*Kahlil Gibran, poet, Lebanon, 1883-1931*

Bring us again, Lord of light,
to that point of trust
    where we know for sure
that before we can even pray
    or make any small promise,
you love us without reservation.
Secure under your smile,
may we step out with humble confidence
    and do what needs be done next
without timidity or fear.
    To your glory, O Christ;
Amen!

*We thank you, holy Father for your holy name, which you have made to live in our hearts, and for the knowledge, faith and immortality which you have revealed to us through your servant Jesus. To you be glory through all ages! Amen.*

*Maria Hare, author, England, 1798-1870*

**August 2**

*One dead fly can make a fragrant ointment stink, and a smidgeon of folly makes wisdom seem putrid.*
> *Qoheleth, 'The Preacher', Ecclesiastes, date unknown*

Loving God,
it is not just my involvement with evil
    that shames and disables me,
it's also my lack of common sense and sensitivity
    which discourages me and wears me down.
God of life, love and enlightenment,
    please continue to have mercy upon me
and salvage the divine spark within me
    from folly, error, and especially from despair.
Amen!

*God, what would it mean*
*to loose our hold*
*let go, put down, give up*
*and walk with empty arms*
*save for the cross of life-affirming death*
*that has been ours*
*since first baptismal breath?*
> *Adapted from Jennie Gordon, UCA minister and poet, Australia,*
> *born 1962*

**August 3**

*Because Jesus said "I am the way", all our journey to heaven is
already heaven.*
                    St. Catherine of Siena, Dominican mystic, Italy, 1347-1380

Blessed and unique are you, Joy of the universe,
   the A and the Z of all things.
Totally authentic are you, God of Jesus,
   without shadow or variation.
Beautiful are you, God of Jesus,
   there is none other as lovely as you.
Patient are you, God in Jesus,
   nothing ever exhausts your loving.
Blessed are you, Joy of the universe,
   you dare make us joint-heirs with Christ!
Hallelujah!

*My thanks, O holy Lord, Father Almighty, Eternal God; Your divine
mercy has kept me safe throughout this day; grant that I pass this
night tranquilly and in cleanness of mind and body, that rising chaste
in the morning hours, I may again render grateful service to you.*
                    Alcuin, scholar and liturgist, England, c. 732-804

**August 4**

*The One God who gave you a soul, also armed you with will power.
Employ it, and you are wise; thus be wise and you will be happy.*
Pharaoh Akhenaton, monotheist, Egypt, c. 1300 BC

Watch over us, faithful Pilot of spaceship earth,
as we hurtle through the cosmos
on the way to things not yet dreamed of.
Help us treat each other kindly
within these confined quarters,
to share the limited provisions and facilities
justly and generously,
and to treat the lowliest person on board
as if they were the ship's Master.
Let us encourage one another
to take time to watch the stars,
to marvel at the work of your fingers,
and to worship with neither
presumption nor pretence.
Through Jesus Christ our Master.
Amen!

*O Lord, you know what is best for me; let this or that be done as you please. Give what you will, how much you will and whenever you will. For your Name's sake. Amen.*
Thomas à Kempis, scholar, Germany, 1380-1471

**August 5**

*To oppress the weak or the meek insults their Maker; to show them mercy is sweet praise to your God.*
                              *Attributed to King Solomon, Jerusalem, c. 950 BC*

Lord of serenity,
    tonight as we prepare for bed
we hand over to you our worries,
    resentments, hurts,
and the sorry failures
    of this long, tiring day.
Let us now possess and enjoy
    that pure spirit of release
which is your gift and pleasure,
    that we may rest in peace
and awake tomorrow
    eager for the new day.
For your names sake.
    Amen!

*O Eternal God, mould us in the crucible of your love so that we become fashioned with the same love you felt when you begat your Son at the first dawn before all creation. For the sake of your Child, Jesus Christ, and lead us to the joy of your salvation.*
                              *Abbess Hildegard of Bingen, mystic-composer, Germany,*
                              *1098-1179*

**August 6**

*Better do a good deed near at home than go far away to burn incense.*

*Amelia Earhart, aviation pioneer, USA, 1897-1937*

Holy Friend,
each day as I grow older,
    please help me to keep in sharp focus
    those visions and dreams of youthful faith;
that vision of your Gospel changing all things,
    like leaven vigorously erupting in dough,
    like a flood-lit city set on a high hill;
that dream of all nations walking hand in hand
    as they 'do justly, love mercy
    and walk humbly with their God'.
Until my final thought and last breath,
    Lord Jesus, keep those visions alive within me.
Amen!

*Everything belongs to God's only Child, all things live in him; through him everything is coming into harmony, in him eternity exists and we are the members of his body. To him, glory and eternity! Amen!*

*Clement of Alexandria, theologian, c. 150 – c. 215*

**August 7**

*Blessed the man or woman who is able to serve cheerfully in the second rank – a big test!*

> *Attributed to Mary Slessor, Scottish Missionary to Nigeria*
> *1848-1915*

True God of True God,
    source of light and holy delight,
how can we reconcile the finality
    which we find in Christ Jesus
with the fruits of the Spirit
    displayed by some other religions?
By your persistent mercies
    deepen our own trust and love,
that we may possess the secure faith
    which will free us to listen to other faiths
without either anxiety or hubris,
and leave the reconciling of all things to you,
the Light of Light, and Joy of Joys.
    Amen!

*Sing, O living Word, of God's love and reveal yourself to my soul; for your word will reach me and your songs will save me. Until now, I was going astray; but ever since you, Lord Jesus, first found me, you have enlightened me and taught me to find God as well. Now I have become an heir at your side, for you are not ashamed to call me your brother. Amen.*

> *Clement of Alexandria, theologian, c. 150 – c. 215*

**August 8**

*Bless Jahweh, O my soul, and all that is within me, bless the holy name.*

*Psalm 103:1, Old Testament*

Blessed are you, God of the mercy-full Jesus,
    you are the Pulse of the universe!
Beyond all earthly power and authority
    reigns your almighty meekness,
    O holy One of Israel!
Beneath all human pity and tenderness
    flows your everlasting strength,
    O holy One of our homeland!
Through all laughter and all tears
    lives your eternal love,
    O holy One of all creation!
Earth and heaven are filled with you glory;
    glory be to you, O Joy most high!
Amen!

*Loving God, as I consider the glory in which I have been created, make me more serious and humble, more deep and cheerful, and more pure and complete as I live my days within your sight. Amen!*

*Thomas Traherne, poet-mystic, England, c. 1637-1674*

**August 9**

*I could not, at any age, be content to take my place in a corner by the fireside and simply look on.*
            *Attributed to Eleanor Roosevelt, politician, USA, 1884-1962*


Loving God, I want to 'put it all on the line for you:'
    all my small faith that it may outscore mundane expectations,
    all my small hope that it may outreach the common grasp,
    all my small love that it may outstrip secular affections.
Keep me as close as possible to your true Son Jesus,
    who freely chose to put it all on the line for you
    and willingly lost the whole lot
    that we might, through him, gain all things.
Amen!


*Hold on to what is good – even if it's a handful of earth.*
*Hold on to what you believe – even if it's a tree that stands by itself.*
*Hold on to where you must go – even if it's a long way from here.*
*Hold on to your life – even if it's easier to let go.*
*Hold on to my hand – even if someday I wander away from you.*
            *Attributed to the Native American Pueblo people, USA,*
                                    *date unknown*

**August 10**

*Those who lose their own dreaming are lost and useless.*
        *Attributed to an Indigenous woman, Australia, date unknown*

Loving Creator-Friend,
    for the playfulness planted within us,
    we give you joyful thanks.
We are grateful for jokes and games;
    for the fun and rejuvenation
    which helps recreate us
and enables us to return
    to our responsibilities
    in a better frame of mind.
Amen!

*O miracle of divine goodness! For these our mortal bodies, you, God, have created all things visible, material, touchable; animals, vegetables and minerals, trees, herbs and flowers, springs, rivers, fountains, oceans, corn, wine and oil, the sun, moon and stars, and the human body – the greatest treasure of all – made for each other! If you give to our mortal bodies such glorious things to enjoy, what then, O Lord, have you prepared for our eternal souls!*
    *Author unknown – maybe Thomas Traherne poet-mystic, England,*
                                    *c. 1637-1674*

**August 11**

*Things are not beautiful in and of themselves. They are merely keys which unlock the beauty hiding inside you.*
*Ellen Willingham Neal, Quoted by Mary C. Nelson,*
*author and publisher, USA, born 1955*

Blessed be your name God.
    O blessed be your name!
As long as there is darkness,
    there will always be a lamp for my feet.
As long as there is a universe,
    there will always be currents of purpose.AD
As long as there are deserts,
    there will always be springs flowing from rocks.
As long as there is human weakness,
    there will always be sufficient grace.
As long as there are valleys in the shadow of death,
    there will always be a rod and staff to comfort me.
Blessed be your name, God.
    O blessed be your name!

*Your Love, O God, is immensely great, great is its overflow. It is never still; always ceaselessly and tirelessly you pour yourself out, so that the small vessel which is our lives, is filled to the brim and overflows into the lives of others. Amen and Amen!*
*Mechthild of Magdeburg, mystic and social activist, Germany,*
*c. 1207 – c. 1282*

**August 12**

*Heavy is a corner stone, weighty a bucket of sand; heavier still is a*
*grudge carried by a fool.*
                        *Attributed to King Solomon, Jerusalem, c. 950 BC*

From the grab-bag of miscellaneous resentments
    and from the heavy baggage of bitter grudges,
    please deliver us, Saviour Christ.
Breathe your merciful Spirit on us again
    that we may forgive others
    as freely as you forgive us,
and so become truly your liberal agents
    of merciful forgiveness
    and apostles of reconciliation.
Amen!

*As I awake from the dark may I be awake to you,*
    *as I rise from my bed may I rise up with you;*
*while I stretch my limbs let me be stretched by you,*
    *as I breathe in the new day may I inhale you.*
*As I flex my hands may they get ready to serve you,*
    *with boots on my feet let me walk with you;*
*as I feed my body may it be strong for you,*
    *while I clear my mind let become full of you.*
                        *Traditional Celtic morning prayer*

**August 13**

*He did not say 'You shall not be tempted, you shall not be travailed and you shall not be diseased' but he said, 'You shalt not be overcome'.*

Lady Julian of Norwich, mystic and theologian, England,
1342-1416

Most faithful God,
   let my faith always be
   held as an holy trust.
Save me from cosy selfishness
   in religious clothing,
and from slick answers
   whenever I am called
   upon to give account
of the creed that inspires and governs
   my going out and my coming in.
Amen!

*God our eternal Saviour, before you each heart is laid bare and every secret thought is uncovered for all souls of the faithful cry out to you. In your loving kindness people put their whole trust; you even hear our silent appeals, and open the gates of mercy to all. Hallelujah!*

Apostolic Constitutions, Syria, c. 375-380

**August 14**

*mercy eats away*
*at our exclusiveness*
*and shouts*
*"come in!"*
                    *Jennie Gordon, UCA minister and poet, Australia, born 1962*

Holy Friend, you know how tricky our minds can be:
you hear us justify prejudices with rational arguments,
    excuse our greed with apparent reasonableness,
    and permit social injustices with calm plausibility.
We are so endemically tricky, Lord,
    that we often don't even realise we are doing it.
Please, rip away the paper masks of corrupted logic,
    that we may better know ourselves,
genuinely repent and become more alert to the evil
    that can contaminate even the sharpest intellect.
Lord in your mercy, hear our prayer.
Amen!

*O Saviour, pour upon me your spirit of meekness and love.*
*Annihilate the wilful-self in me; be my whole life. Guide my hand*
*which trembles exceedingly upon the rock of ages.*
                    *William Blake, poet and artist, England, 1757-1827*

**August 15**

*For me, the one essential link between me and everything else can only be found in Jesus, the man from Nazareth, whose mystery is more revealing than all the far more precise explanations, rationales and arguments of any other age or experience.*
*Robert Renton, UCA minister and educationalist, Australia,*
*born 1946*

Lord of laughter, open our eyes to see through the
    absurdities of this brazen new age without despairing.
Help us to smile while the very wealthy whinge
    and the politicians strut and dissemble.
Give us the grace to chuckle at technological vain-glory
    or the self-praise of the entertainment industry.
When a little knowledge poses as a scientific fact,
    enable us to laugh heartily with the faith born at Easter.
And, Lord of laughter, when we take ourselves too seriously,
    laugh at us until we come to our senses.
For your love's sake;
    Amen!

*God, of your goodness, give me yourself; for you are sufficient for me. I cannot properly ask anything less, to be worthy of you. If I were to ask less, I would always be in want. In you alone do I have all. Amen.*
*Lady Julian of Norwich, mystic and theologian, England,*
*1342-1416*

**August 16**

*Speak up for those whose voices are not heard, stand up for the social minnows and misfits.*
      *Attributed to Lemuel, King of Massa, Middle East, c. 400-200 BC*


Immortal Love, rest your suffering ones
      upon pillows of divine compassion,
and with fingers of supreme tenderness
      dislodge the seeds of disease;
throughout daylight hours
      encircle them with human kindness,
and in the long, sleepless nights of illness
      surround them with the Light
      which nothing can smother.
Amen!


*Please give us, Father-God, a clean start for beginners, wisdom to the young and aid to those who are running hard, repentance to those who fall, a revived fire to the lukewarm, and to those who have given their best a good ending. Amen.*
      *St. Irenaeus, Bishop of Lyons, France, c. 200*

**August 17**


*Far better to be a free termite than a caged dingo.*
                               *Indigenous elder, Australia, contemporary*


Holy Friend,
we pray for all who caught in a secret bondage:
     the captives of nightmares or crippling anxieties,
slaves to drugs or compulsive behaviours,
     drudges to power freaks or sexual harassment,
those addicted to pornography or violence,
     young folk trapped by anorexia and bulimia,
and those who are victims of spiritual bullies
     or who are indoctrinated with religious terrors.
Please help them to seek and accept wise counsel,
     and come to know the liberty of the Spirit.
Through your saving grace and to your glory.
     Amen!


*Save us, O lord, while waking, and guard us while sleeping; that
when we awake we may watch with Christ, and when we sleep we
may rest in his peace.*
                               *Adapted from the Roman Catholic breviary*

**August 18**

*By the constancy of the Holy Spirit, a lovely rose can grow on a humble thorn.*
> *Mechthild of Magdeburg, mystic and social activist, Germany,*
> *c. 1207 – c. 1282*

Holy Friend,
    you are the life of my living
    the joy of my laughing
    the faith of my believing
    and the death of my dying.
Help me so to love you that
    my trust may ever be grounded in you,
    my service be ever shaped by you,
    my ageing may be content in you,
and my death may make me complete with you.
Amen!

*With the hosts of heaven we join in praising you, O Lord; we who are your frail, weak and lowly servants thank you for your grace for which we cannot make an adequate return. You have clothed yourself in our humanity that you might give us life through your own divinity. You have exalted our lowliness, raised us up from where we had fallen, and brought us back to the fullness of life.*
> *Responsory of Addai and Mari, East Syria, c. 410*

**August 19**

*I am no caged bird; and no net ensnares me; I am a free spirit with
an independent will.*

> Charlotte Bronte, writer, England, 1816-1855


Like a song bird
    basking in early morning sunshine
or an excited small child
    dancing in the fringes of the ocean,
help each of us, loving God,
    to bask with uninhibited leisure
and to dance with utter delight
    in the luxury of your abundant grace
given to us in Christ Jesus.
Amen!


*Creator of heaven and earth, you adorn the skies with the choir of
stars and fill up the earth with good fruits for the health of us all.
your kindness grant to the human race, which you have raised up
from the dust, to rejoice with the brilliance of the stars and to be
nourished by the fruits of the earth. Through your only begotten
son, Jesus Christ. Amen.*

> Serapion, Bishop of Thmuis, Egypt, c. 350

**August 20**

*It is only through the unity of God that a society can cohere into a true community.*

*P.T. Forsyth, theologian, England, 1848-1921*

God of the downtrodden and the poor,
   let your light and love rest with profusion
   on your beloved indigenous people.
Guide those who are strong in spirit
   to give a wise and bold leadership
   that won't capitulate to apathy.
Channel the anger of the desperate
   into creative plans for reform.
Surround with your deep healing grace
   those who are broken and lost.
And, in your patient mercies,
   send some modern Amos to the rest of us
lest we stagnate in indifference to injustice
   and finally perish in our willfulness.
         Amen!

*The pilgrim God with shoulders broad, support the burden of my load.*
*The wounded Christ searching for me, hear my cry at end of day.*
*The caring Sister Spirit of truth, guide my steps when I am late.*

*Traditional Celtic prayer*

**August 21**

*The Cross was the earthy pole of an act within the heavenly Godhead. If our thinking does not allow for that belief, we reduce faith to something plain, boring, and songless. Making faith more homely renders it much less holy, less absolute, less adoring.*

*P.T. Forsyth, theologian, England, 1848-1921*

You who are the Deep Calm,
    hush my cyclonic anxieties.
Deep calm of the Creator's hand,
    quieten my nervous body.
Deep calm of the Teacher from Galilee,
    silence my agitated mind.
Deep calm of the Spirit of truth,
    still my trembling soul.
Possess me with your purpose
    and hug me in the arms of your peace.
Amen!

*O Lord, you have taught us that whatever is done without love is useless. Please send your Holy Spirit and pour into our hearts that most excellent gift of 'agape' which is the very bond of peace and of all other virtues, for without love we might as well be dead. Grant this, for your Son Jesus Christ's sake.*
*Amen.*
   *Thomas Cranmer, Archbishop of Canterbury, England, 1489-1556*

**August 22**

*An ass may bray a long while yet never shake the stars down.*
*Mary Anne Evans (pen name George Eliot) novelist and journalist,*
*England, 1819-1880*

There are times, O God when, like old Job,
    I get angry with you for this dysfunctional world
where suffering is wantonly perpetrated
    by the rich and powerful against the poor and weak,
with torture, bombings, mugging, domestic violence,
    hunger, homelessness, starvation, massacres!
"For Christ's sake", I cry out,
    "wasn't there a better way
to set up your creation than this?
    If your Name truly is both wisdom and love
is this really the best possible world?"

*Be present, O merciful God and protect us through the silent hours*
*of this dark night, so that we who are wearied by the changes and*
*chances of this fleeting world may repose in your eternal*
*changelessness. Through Jesus Christ our Lord. Amen.*
*Leonine Prayers, Rome, 5th century*

**August 23**

*'Electric' communication will never be a substitute for the face to face meeting of someone who with their soul encourages another person to be brave and true.*

*Charles Dickens, novelist, England, 1812-1870*

For the many blessings of 'virtual reality',
    we give you thanks, Lord of all life;
But keep us in touch with your Reality, O God;
    save us and enhance us by your truth;
Knit us to the real Christ in others,
    that we may seek first your righteous love
and enter into that un-anxious joy
    which has been prepared for us
since the foundation of the world.
Amen!

*Saviour God, we pray for this people: Send upon them the Holy Spirit, that the Lord Jesus himself may come and visit them, speaking with the spirit of each, and preparing their hearts to receive larger faith. Amen.*

*Serapion, Bishop of Thmuis, Egypt, c. 350*

**August 24**

*I am among those who think that science has great beauty. A scientist in his laboratory is not only a technician: he is also a child placed before natural phenomena which impress him like a fairy tale.*
*Madame Curie, scientist, France, 1867-1934*

God of sun, moon, space shuttles and communication satellites,
    of dinosaurs, pelicans, cloned cows and IVF,
help us to worship you in spirit and in truth,
    not only in prayers but also in our daily work and leisure.

God of bellbird, didgeridoo, guitar and symphony orchestra,
    of camel trains, chariots, passenger jets and bullet trains,
help us to worship you in spirit and in truth,
    not only in prayers but also in our choices and commitments
Amen!

*How thankful I am, O God, that you know me better than I know myself, and you allow me to know myself better than those around me. Please make me, I beg you – God the all-merciful – better than they think I am, and forgive me the evil they do not know.*
*Attributed to Abu Bekr, mystic, Syria, c. 620*

**August 25**

*Free grace is the basis of God's saving justice; his radical kind of*
*'justification' is found in dining with tax collectors and sinners.*
                    *Magda Christopher, feminist author, Australia, born 1987*

God of infinite tenderness,
    enfold your bride, the church,
    in your sure, caring arms
    and heal its many wounds.
Let trust replace anxiety,
    humility unseat pride,
    and love supplant enmity.
Grant to your people
    the inner peace of the Christ
    that reconciles and renews all.
In the name of Jesus, our Saviour,
    Amen!

*You, God are the Subject of my joys and the Object of my work, yet I*
*cannot shake off all the negative habits which the lost years have*
*wrought in me. I can only ask of you to have mercy on me, and*
*subdue in me everything that is perverse and wayward. So fill me*
*with your pure graciousness, that my narrowness sand selfishness*
*may be all done away with in the immense wideness of your love.*
*Amen.*
                    *The Didache, 'The Teachings', Syria, c. 120*

**August 26**

*I am your God and your Maker who watches over you in the silence; your friend, your shelter, and your peaceful home.*
                    *Bhagavad Gita, Hindu Scriptures, India, c. 600 BC*

Bless to me
    this body which is my friend,
    this mind which explores many things,
    and this soul with which I know your love.
Bless to me
    my ears, that I may listen openly,
    my voice, that I may speak wisely,
    my face, that I may smile freely.
Bless to me
    these fingers with which I write,
    these arms with which I hug,
    these feet with which I move.
God of great faithfulness,
    bless all that is within me,
    and all who live around me,
    with the grace that knows no ending.
Amen!

*God, by love alone you are great and glorious. Help us, we pray, by loving to attain another self, by loving to live in others, and through loving finally come to look upon your glory and accompany your love throughout all eternity.*
                    *Thomas Traherne, poet-mystic, England, c. 1637-1674*

**August 27**

*All shall be well, and all shall be well, and all manner of things shall be well.*

> *Lady Julian of Norwich, mystic and theologian, England,*
> *1342-1416*

Thank you, Lord Jesus, for linking us together
    in the fellowship of your church;
where we can find those honest enough to help us
    recognise our own follies and biases,
and where we can learn to assist others
    without patronising them,
and to help the needy without humiliating them,
    to forgive as we are forgiven,
and to be all things to all people
    by meekly serving without qualification.
Through Christ Jesus, our masterly servant.
Amen!

*Bless me, O God, with the gift of love for you and my neighbour. Give me the serenity of integrity and keep me in control of word and deeds. Your will be done, Giver of grace, mercy and peace.*

> *Thomas Wilson, Bishop, Isle of Man, 1663-1755*

**August 28**

*I believe that banking institutions are more dangerous to our liberties than standing armies.*
>            Thomas Jefferson, third President of the USA, 1743-1826

Source of all good government,
    the God of all races and countries,
give our national leaders the vision to see through
    the big challenges of the days ahead.
Show them the best way to develop
    the higher gifts of all citizens
and to foster more opportunities
    for the weak, the neglected, and the inept,
that all may walk with assurance
    and dignity among the nations,
with neither arrogance nor avarice,
    in the ministry of reconciliation and peace.
Amen!

*Lord, what a change within us one short hour spent in your presence makes; what burdens can be lifted, what ground can be refreshed, when we kneel down in weakness, so that we can stand up strong.*
>        Adapted from Archbishop Trench, theologian, Dublin, 1807-1886

**August 29**

*in order to emerge*
*you must descend*
*in order to begin*
*you'll face the end.*
                    Jennie Gordon, UCA minister and poet, Australia, born 1962

Merciful and patient God,
    I know that I often fail to be
    the kind of friend my friends do need.
But in spite of my many faults,
    I pray for this one special thing:
that notwithstanding my many failings
    they may clearly see a little
of your gospel at work in me,
    and have cause to thank the Spirit
who is the very Joy of the universe
    and the Friend of sinners.
Amen!

*God, the benefactor of all races, you make the light to shine on all*
*faces; you give growth to every mustard seed and cause all to*
*blossom and grow. Holy are you; holy are you, who from my youth*
*have shone your light and given me your life. Amen.*
                    *From a fragment (klasmata) of early Christian papyrus*

**August 30**

*I have less material things than ever. I don't even have a car. I don't own a home. Yet I couldn't be happier.*
> *Scott Neeson, contemporary philanthropist and worker*
> *with street kids in Cambodia, born 1959*


We pray, God of the servant Christ,
    for big business and big unions
    throughout our nation:
Give them the genuine desire and will
    to listen to each other;
and give them the needed humility
    to accept how much they need
    each other to maintain prosperity.
For your mercy's sake;
    Amen!


*O God, we all stand before you in our differences, yet alike in that we are all in the wrong with you and with one another and that we would all be lost without the saving grace you have made available to us in your dear Son. By your grace we are here wanting to praise you through letting you speak to us and through us; in the name of your Son, our Lord. Amen.*
> *Adapted from Karl Barth, theologian, Switzerland, 1886-1968*

**August 31**

*Happy are those who are found to be walking in the ways of Christ;*
*the second death shall have no power over them.*

St. Francis of Assisi, friar, Italy, 1181-1226

Most awesome Friend,
in theory we acknowledge that you can use
our handicaps and faults for your purposes;
but in practice we are neither eager to admit
the deficiencies we do have
nor ready to entrust them to you.
Please override our silly pride;
we entrust our handicaps to you
and pray for that special grace
which is made perfect
in our human weaknesses.
To your praise and the growth of your realm
here on earth, we pray.
Amen!

*O Lord, you command your loving kindness in the daytime, and in*
*the night declare the same, we ask you please to preserve us*
*throughout this long day and tonight guard our rest; through Jesus*
*Christ our Lord. Amen.*

Spanish prayer, c. 6th-11th century

**September 1**

*He is our Lord Jesus Christ, who brings under judgement all petty human loyalties and transforms them into the life of the Kingdom of God, in which we may know and enjoy him forever.*
                              *David Beswick, UCA minister and psychologist, Australia,*
                                                                        *born 1933*

Loving God,
many of us say we live in a city
because, we claim,
"that is where the action is".

Help us to make sure
that the action
of which we speak
is aligned with your action.
Amen!

*Author of all marvels, we praise you. Creator of all things heavenly and earthly, we praise you. Your power and your wisdom are everywhere displayed. You have placed the night skies to be a roof over our heads, and the solid and fruitful earth to be the ground under our feet. O Father and Guardian of humankind, we thank and praise you! Now and for ever. Amen.*
                     *Based on Caedmon, Christian poet, Northumbria, 6th century*

**September 2**

*As a single footstep will not make a path on the earth, so a single thought will not make a pathway in the mind. To make a deep mental path, we must think over and over the kind of thoughts we wish to dominate our lives.*

*Henry David Thoreau, philosopher, USA, 1817-1862*

O Son of Man, firstborn of a new breed,
    please induct us into your new world
    where no member is superior
    and no one is ever superfluous;
where mercy and justice embrace
    and love has the first and final say;
    for your name's sake.
Amen!

*God, the Father of all, you have lovingly made the peoples of the world to be one family. Help those of different races and religions to love, understand and accept one another. Take away all hatred, jealousy and prejudice, so that all may work together for the coming of your kingdom of righteousness and peace; through Jesus Christ our Lord. Amen!*

*Evelyn Underhill, author and mystic, England, 1875-1941*

**September 3**

*I may sit on a peasant's back, half-choking him and making him carry me, and yet assure myself and others that I am very sorry for him and wish to ease his lot by all possible means — except by getting off his back.*

*Leo Tolstoy, novelist, Russia, 1828-1910*

Loving God, embrace all your suffering ones
    with your almighty tenderness.
Where the natural healing forces are weak,
    or where the agents of decay are strong,
grant an infusion of your healing love,
    penetrating every cell and tissue
and recreating health and well-being.
    Through your true Son,
the wounded Lord who lives with us
    everywhere and forever.
    Amen!

*O giver of life, let us dislodge from our minds the fantasy that would make bringing much joy to you to be something other than the deeds we do for others.*

*Rabindranath Tagore, poet, India, 1861-1941*

**September 4**

*We fear our small boat is alone, rowed through the blackest night,*
*then from the open sea comes the splash of other paddles.*
                                    *Anonymous, Japan, 8th century*

God of innumerable gifts,
      thanks for the incognito Christ
who shares our journey
      through every moment,
challenging our foolishness,
      forgiving our faithlessness,
nursing our injuries,
      blessing our strengths,
and making our cup overflow
      with cheerfulness and goodwill.
Amen!

*May the warm winds of Heaven blow softly upon your house*
*and may the Great Spirit bless all who enter there.*
*May your moccasins make happy tracks in many snows*
*and may the rainbow always touch your shoulder.*
                          *Cherokee blessing, Native American, date unknown*

**September 5**

*If my words teach the public that men are made mad by bad treatment, and if the police are taught that they may exasperate to madness men they persecute and ill-treat, my life will not be entirely thrown away,*
            *Ned Kelly, iconic 'bushranger', Australia, executed 1880*

Giver of light, we are identical in our need
      of your forgiveness and guidance.
We all know what it is like to lose our way;
      each has their own story of sin and regret.
Yet we are never hope-less;
      together we trust the one Saviour
      and drink from the same well of salvation.
Thank you, Saviour God.
      Amen!

*Lord Jesus, you did not zoom in upon us as if from another planet, but born like us, you grew day by day, attended school, and went on pilgrimages to holy places and listened to holy men. Thank you, loving God, for not allowing his name to be lost in oblivion, but you raised him up the very highest in your realm of eternal loving. Amen.*
            *Ron Gordon, UCA minister and writer, Australia, born 1932*

**September 6**

*Faith is the grand venture in which we commit our whole soul, and
all our future, to the confidence that Christ is not an illusion but the
sure reality of God.*

*P.T. Forsyth, theologian, England, 1848-1921*

God of Eternal Light,
    by the healing fingers of the Lord Jesus,
Please take the scales of bigotry from my eyes
    until I begin to glimpse you in alien faces,
and unstop my intolerant ears
    that I may sometimes hear your Word
    in other faiths or in secular converse.
For your Name's sake.
    Amen!

*Holy One, you are the Persian, Buddhist and Sikh, the Church of Ma
Thoma and Hindu. You are the man, the woman and child, the pan
flute player and the herdsman with cows. You are the fount of life,
and the giver of love, the source of prosperity and the giver of
yourself. Everywhere and in all shapes you are dear to me, yet
always you remain your very own Self. You alone are my creed, my
beginning and my end.*

*Gobind Singh, Sikh Guru, India, 1666-1708*

**September 7**

*May the Lord Jesus continue to speak through us, and may the Holy
Spirit celebrate God in us with songs of joy.*
                                        *Serapion, Bishop of Thmuis, Egypt, c. 350*


Still you come again to us, Christ Jesus,
    to help us discover opals of your truth embedded
    deeper than twitter, advertiser's wiles, or political spin.
Still you come again among us,
    not as a ghost from the past but as the Spirit of the future,
    offering us more than we can ask or as yet receive.
We delight in your coming, Lord Jesus,
    as we seek to follow you today better than yesterday.
    To the glory of God and the enrichment of the earth.
Amen!


*God, make each moment of our lives a miracle; make us laugh at
the utterly impossible and give us hope when all things seem
hopeless. Grant us the precious gift of peace where no peace should
be likely, and love for the unlovable. Make us to wager all on your
providence, and to dare everything in your service. Amen!*
                                        *Adelaide E. Procter, poet, England, 1825-1864*

**September 8**

*All tyranny needs to gain a foothold is for people of good conscience to remain silent.*
>                          *Thomas Jefferson, third President of the USA, 1743-1826*

Rescue us, faithful God,
    from putting either too much hope
    or investing too little faith
    in political programs and leaders.
Help us, like good stewards, to use
    that small, vital influence we do have
to help make our political system work
    for the good of all citizens.
    Amen!

*Bless us, O God, in this breakfast meal,*
*strength for the body and for the mind.*
*Give us, O God, of your milk and honey,*
*strength for spirit all day long.*

*Bless us, O God, as by candlelight*
*we eat meat for our weary flesh.*
*Give us, O God, of your very Self,*
*chalice of love that never ends.*

>                                    *Traditional Celtic table grace*

**September 9**

*True wisdom is less presuming than folly. The wise man doubts often, and may change his mind. The fool is obstinate and doubts not; he recognises all things but his own ignorance.*
                    *Pharaoh Akhenaton, monotheist, Egypt, c. 1300 BC*

Go out into the world in peace,
    let nothing dismay you
    and no fear betray you.
Put your trust in the God
    who knows your needs even
    before you ask for aid,
and will not allow any good thing
    which you have vowed and done
    to finally be pilfered or mislaid.
Amen!

*Holy and beautiful are you, Creator Spirit; now at the hour of sunset as we gaze at the soft evening light, we sing to the Father and to the Son and to the Holy Spirit, our thanksgiving and praise for the day that is now passing into night. Amen!*
                    *From a fragment (klasmata) of early Christian papyrus*

**September 10**

*You are now on the right track, which is the most beautiful path as well, therefore run fearlessly that race of faith.*
> *Cyril, Bishop of Jerusalem, theologian, c. 313 – c. 386*

Holy Friend, joy of the universe,
    you are the fire in the belly of your saints
    and the light in the eyes of children;
please grant us the grace and sanity
    to willingly learn from them
    how to will-fully 'lay it all on the line' for you.
Deliver us from the blind sophistication
    of those who make an easy truce
    with the gods of mammon and hubris.
Return us to the sane, childhood of faith,
    where things that go largely unseen
    are more real than things that are seen;
For your love's sake.
Amen!

*Let our body be a servant of our mind, and both body and spirit servants of Jesus Christ; that doing all things for thy glory here, we may be partakers of thy glory hereafter; through the same Jesus Christ our Lord.*
> *Jeremy Taylor, priest and author, England 1613-1667*

**September 11**

*The child's sob curses deeper in the silence than the strong man in his wrath.*

*Elizabeth Browning, poet, England, 1806-1861*

For children who go to school hungry
    because parents gamble their family benefits cheque,
for teenage refugees who are locked in detention camps,
    waiting for their cases to be processed:
we pray to the God of hope and liberation.

For children who against their will, or out of dire necessity,
    are exploited in pornography and the sex trade,
for the bewildered and abused among young indigenes
    who resort to sniffing petrol or smashing shop windows.
we pray to the God of hope and liberation.
    Lord have mercy; Christ have mercy; Lord have mercy.
Amen!

*O God, you have chosen to make us your playmates; please lead the child within each of us in your just and caring ways. May we love mercy, doing it gladly and steadfastly, and so become like you in your compassionate deeds. Amen.*

*Mechthild of Magdeburg, mystic and social activist, Germany, c. 1207 – c. 1282*

**September 12**

*He whose head is always in the clouds will never reap any harvest.*
*Qoheleth, 'The Preacher', Ecclesiastes, date unknown*

If young desert oaks spend years
    putting down sixty metre roots
    before showing much above ground,
how much more should we be willing to
    to patiently put down deep roots
    into the very Ground of our being
and search out the deeper Springs
    of the eternal water of Life;
    O God our hope and our happiness!
Amen!

*What shall I render unto God for all these blessings? I can only give*
*my own self, all I have and am; have pity on me, poor and needy as*
*I am. Subdue in me that which is mean and rebellious in my heart*
*and so fill me with your pure and heavenly love, that all my*
*narrowness may be done away with in the wideness of your*
*mercies; for your Name's sake. Amen.*
*Maria Hare, author, England, 1798-1870*

**September 13**

*Any religion which sacrifices women to the brutality of men is no true religion.*

*Julia Ward Howe, poet and abolitionist, USA, 1819-1910*

Loving God,
    we repent the ways in which we have allowed
gender discrimination to deride
    and degrade our human dignity.
May each of us, women and men, girls and boys,
    do more affirming and less demoralising;
Let the rising tide of mutual respect and concern,
    which your Spirit is creating in this new age,
attain your justice with a beauty and balance
    that will restore some esteem in us,
and love, worship and delight in you.
Amen!

*God my Dearest, I thank you for making me like yourself, so that my 'femaleness' is a reflection of an aspect of your bountiful Being. Please encourage me to maintain a high respect for myself, to rejoice in all that is lovely and divinely human in my womanhood.*

*Magda Christopher, feminist author, Australia, born 1987*

**September 14**

*Being a Christian can be tough when you are among your friends at school, but it can also be fun and worthwhile.*

*Twelve-year-old boy, Australia, date unknown*

God, the *Abba* of Jesus and our Father,
    be to my adult children
the wise and truly loving parent
    I never was or ever could be.
Guide them, and their growing families,
    throughout this day's hassles and happiness
and give them, sweeter than honeycomb,
    a taste of Your Presence.
Amen!

*Christ be with me, Christ before me,*
*Christ be after me, Christ within me,*
*Christ beneath me, Christ above me,*
*Christ at my right, Christ at my left,*
*Christ in the home, Christ on the road,*
*Christ in the heart of everyone who thinks of me.*
*Christ in the mouth of everyone who speaks with me.*
*Christ in every eye that sees me.*
*Christ in every ear that listens to me.*

*St. Patrick, Ireland, 387-461*

**September 15**

*All ambitions are lawful except those which climb upward on the miseries or credulities of mankind.*
*Joseph Conrad, Polish-English author, England, 1857-1924*

Joy of loving hearts,
    whenever I tremble on the brink
    of a most difficult decision.
Save me from being taken in
    by superficial appearances
    or by subtle self-deceits.
Give me a clear head,
    a strong and persistent will,
    and a serene heart.
By your enabling grace
    and to your service and praise.
Amen!

*Almighty Giver of all good, may our hearts sing with gratitude for the overwhelming number of blessings you have showered upon us. Make us to sing your song of love and thanks in the morning and in the night feel the touch of your hand and be at peace. May you be our trusted Lord for evermore. Amen.*
*Henry W. Foote, Presbyterian minister, USA, 1794-1869*

**September 16**

*You find us
in the midst of our routine lives
doing what we always do
and frighten us
with tremendous glory*
        *Jennie Gordon, UCA minister and poet, Australia, born 1962*


Holy, most holy Friend, enable us
    to adore you without restraint,
to serve you without complaint,
    to be in awe of you without fear,
and to know you when you appear,
    For your love's sake.
Amen!


*Source of all blessings, we thank you: for the air that gives the breath of life, the sun that warms us, and the good food that makes us strong; for happy homes and for the friends we love; for health and vigour and all that makes it good to be alive. Make us thankful and eager to repay, by cheerfulness and by a readiness to help others. Freely we have received, let us freely give; in the name of him who gave his life for us; Jesus Christ our Lord.*
    *Bishop Thomas Ken, cleric and hymn writer, England, 1637-1711*

**September 17**


*greed creeps*
*  in soft socks*
*so as not to wake*
*  our sleeping soul*
                 *Jennie Gordon, UCA minister and poet, Australia, born 1962*



You, God, see the unheeded suffering
    of innumerable people,
    and you hear the private sobbing
    of countless children;
O let your breath be upon all you see,
    your merciful hands upon all disease,
    your everlasting arms around all distress,
    and your kiss of peace on all tormented minds;
for your love's sake.
Amen!



*God our Father, we know we are weak-willed and feel we are not*
*built for gallant undertakings in your name. Please, replace our*
*weakness with your strength, that we may do far better in the*
*spiritual battles of our times; arm us against our own sloppiness*
*and spinelessness, and defend us from the sneakiness of our own*
*traitorous feelings. For Jesus Christ's sake. Amen.*
                 *Thomas à Kempis, scholar, Germany, 1380-1471*

**September 18**


*The marvels of God are not brought forth by one's self. Rather, it is more like a chord, a sound that is played. The tone does not come out of the instrument by itself, but rather, through the touch of the Musician. I am, of course, merely a harp of God's kindness.*
*Abbess Hildegard of Bingen, mystic-composer, Germany,*
*1098-1179*


Greenescent in the evening sunlight,
    a flock of lorikeets jet low over housetops
    aiming for the next clump of gum trees.
Lord, their native mastery of flight
    makes me yearn and pray for
    a similar spiritual skill and mastery
in this heavenly environment of dailyness
    in which you have placed me
    to live and move and have my being.
Loving Creator, hear my prayer.
Amen!


*O Lord, look on me: here you see goodness, here you see evil; take them both from me and grant me nothing but love of you. Here you see knowledge, here you see ignorance; take them both from me and grant me nothing but love of you.*
*Ramakrishna, mystic, India, 1836-1886*

**September 19**

*There is a [regrettable] tendency on the local church scene to turn Christianity into a programme for becoming successful in the world; Christian faith is then extolled as the best strategy for being a social success.*
        *Norman Young, minister and theologian, Australia, born 1930*

Strong, Saviour-Christ,
        please continue to save us from 'experts'
        who babble at us from TV, Twitter and Radio;
From know-alls who approach every question with an open mouth,
        from those who push theories as if they were immutable laws,
from those who extol market forces as if they were benign agents,
        from experts who preach personal greed as a cardinal virtue,
        from those who push aside ethical questions with opinion polls,
        and from the arrogant who leave no space for humility or doubt,
deliver us, Jesus, our will-full freedom and delight.
Amen!

*O Lord, because we often sin and have to ask for pardon, help us to forgive as we would be forgiven; neither mentioning old offences committed against us, nor dwelling upon in thought but loving others freely as you so freely love us; for your name's sake. Amen.*
        *Christina Rossetti, poet, England, 1830-1894*

**September 20**


*Christian optimism refuses to bow to present disasters. It enables a man to hold his head high, to claim the future for himself and not to abandon it to the enemy.*

Author unknown


Though this body become weak,
    let us be strong in you.
Though the mind grow stiff,
    let us be young in you.
Though faith become frail,
    let us be robust in you.
Through your faithfulness.
    we can do all things!
Amen!


*It is right God, that we should sing your praises, and be glad and happy with you! You are the Spirit Supreme, the creator and saviour of the world. You are from before the beginning, and beyond the end, the ultimate Treasure of the universe, the Knower of all who seeks to be known. O you who are before and behind us, adoration is yours. O you who are within and beyond us, adoration is yours. O you who are the hope and the seed, the flower, fruit and the harvest consummation; adoration is yours!*

Bhagavad Gita, Hindu Scriptures, India, c. 600 BC

**September 21**

*Never lose an opportunity for seeing anything that is beautiful; For beauty is God's handwriting, a wayside sacrament . . . and I thank God for it as a cup of His blessing.*
> Ralph Waldo Emerson, poet-philosopher, USA, 1803-1882

God, our Holy Friend,
    bless us with Christ's generous spirit.
May we be numbered among the merciful;
    not straining to do the right thing out of fear,
but offering love from a heart that cherishes
    your persistent mercy towards us.
For that we earnestly pray,
    and to that we thoroughly commit.
So help me God!
Amen!

*O Lord, we thank you for this new day with its new strength and vigour, its new hopes and its new opportunities. Help us to meet its joys with praise, its difficulties with fortitude, and its duties with fidelity. Grant us wisdom and clear vision. Direct our steps and guard us from error. And of your great mercy deliver us from evil; through Jesus Christ our Lord.*
> H. Bisseker, priest, England, 1878-?

**September 22**

*God answers sharp and sudden on some prayers, and thrusts the thing*
*we have prayed for back in our face; a gauntlet with a gift in it.*
                                        *Elizabeth Browning, poet, England, 1806-1861*

O strong, inexorable Stirrer,
    confront and discomfort your church.
Work relentlessly in us lest we lose touch
    with the very Gospel which we salute with our creeds,
    praise with our hymns and preach from our pulpits.
For your love's sake.
    Amen!

*The peace of God, our only peace,*
*the peace of Columba, kindly peace,*
*the peace of Mary, generous and kind,*
*the peace of Christ, king of tenderness;*
*yes, the peace of Christ, king of tenderness:*

*Rest upon each window and each door,*
*upon each space that lets light in,*
*upon the four corners of my house,*
*upon the four corners of my bed,*
*yes, rest on the four corners of my bed.*

*The peace of God, true earthly peace,*
*the peace of Christ, king of tenderness,*
*rest on my body made of dust,*
*rest on my spirit from on high,*
*yes, rest on my spirit from on high.*

                                        *Traditional Celtic prayer*

**September 23**

*Human beings have not woven the web of life, we are but one thread within it. Whatever we do to the web, we do to ourselves; all things are bound together.*

*Attributed to Chief Seattle, Suquamish Native American, USA, c. 1786-1866*

So that our little days
    may even now participate
    in your eternal day,
loving God, open our hands and hearts
    to receive more of your love
    and liberally to share it.
Through Jesus, our first love
    and the deathless joy of the universe;
Amen!

*The teeming creation is your handiwork, Eternal God, and what is most wonderful, you place human beings here. In us you brought into existence a world within a world; we emerge from nothingness to exercise reason and judgment, faith and love, within this paradise of delights. To you our praise and our hymns, to you all honour and glory, God and Father, through the Son and in the Holy Spirit, for ever and ever. Amen!*

*Apostolic Constitutions, Syria, c. 375-380*

**September 24**

*The soul is deeply kissed by God, as grace and blessing are
bestowed to take on God's gentle yoke. It is the sweetest thing to
give one's self to God's Way.*

*Abbess Hildegard of Bingen, mystic-composer, Germany,
1098-1179*

God of Moses, and of Jesus,
    you are the enemy of those contemporary idols
which fascinate and corrupt humanity;
    please have mercy on each and all of us.
Before it is too late, put paid to our allegiance to electronic idols;
    shatter our addiction to video screens, smart phones,
    key boards, icons and exotic software.
Grind the golden calf of our contemporary idolatry
    into an unpalatable dust;
awaken in us once more that primeval awe and delight
    which is the indigenous worship of our spirits.
Through Christ Jesus our sure Redeemer.
    Amen!

*Holy Jesus, give me the gift and spirit of prayer; outreach my
ignorances, passionate desires, and imperfect choices with your
grace, that my truest needs may be fulfilled.*

*Jeremy Taylor, priest and author, England 1613-1667*

**September 25**

*Be kind to all, for everyone you meet is fighting their own hard battle.*
  *Philo of Alexandria, Jewish philosopher, Greece, c. 20 BC – c. 50 AD*

O Spirit of relentless mercies,
    if you were quick to take offence,
    you would have discarded us long ago.
We thank you for your patience,
    your tolerance and generosity,
    your insistent and healing forgiveness;
for your gentle and thorough nurturing
    of those gifts, so often fragile,
    which we all have within us.
To your praise and glory;
Amen!

*Give us a hand, dear Master, and lift us up; make us stand tall, may our eyes be lifted up to you and let our eyes be wide open. Give us confidence; do not let us be shamed, confused, or to constantly put ourselves down; for you have cancelled the decree against us, and written our names in your book of life. To you be glory and power, now and for ever and ever. Amen.*
                    *Serapion, Bishop of Thmuis, Egypt, c. 350*

**September 26**

*All I have seen teaches me to trust the Creator for all I have not seen.*
*Ralph Waldo Emerson, poet-philosopher, USA, 1803-1882*

Here, loving Creator,
    in this Outback wilderness
    we start noticing and cherishing
the exquisite beauty
    of tiny desert flowers,
    of quiet, cool waterholes,
    and of ordinary people.
O God of the wilderness,
    Creator and Provider,
    Saviour and Enabler,
    we bless our good fortune!
Amen!

*Praise be to you, O Christ: though creator, you became a man,*
*though law giver, you submitted to it, though good shepherd, you*
*became a sheep; though high priest, you became the sacrifice:*
*Blessed is your name in all the earth. Amen.*
*Apostolic Constitutions, Syria, c. 375-380*

**September 27**

*My complaint is that so much of our inculcated piety is flabby; an over simplified Christ becomes pietistic white-wash.*
                    *P.T. Forsyth, theologian, England, 1848-1921*


Come, Dayspring from on high,
come to your own,
and fashion a generation
of seers.
    Spread the dawn
    over grey horizons
    and prepare eyes
    for the first light.
        Come as you came
        on a cloud of yesterdays
        and touch to life
        our mortal dust.


*Help us, good Lord, to serve another gladly and to forgive each other from the bottom of our hearts. Lord God, heavenly Father, who has bound us together in one body through your Holy Spirit, help us, we beg you, to serve one another though Jesus Christ our Lord. Amen.*
            *Thomas Bradwardine, theologian and mathematician, England,*
                                *1290-1349*

**September 28**

*I do not feel obliged to believe that the same God who has endowed us with sense, reason, and intellect has intended us to forgo their use.*

*Galileo Galilei, astronomer, Italy, 1564-1642*

Holy Spirit, Bird of Paradise,
come and cover us with your motherly wings,
    warming cold hearts, healing wounded bodies,
    and dispelling our guilty fears.
Generous Giver and Holy Abundance,
    endow us with whatever gifts you choose,
and inspire us to employ such gifts astutely,
    not as a slave's duty, but as our free delight.
Through Jesus Christ our Lord.
Amen!

*Lord Jesus Christ, you alone are wisdom, you know what is best for us; mercifully grant that it may happen in ways that are pleasing to you, and as seems good this day; for your Name's sake. Amen.*

*King Henry VI, England, 1421-1471*

**September 29**

*I, your God, am the only wisdom of the wise and the sole beauty of
the beautiful.*

*Bhagavad Gita, Hindu Scriptures, India, c. 600 BC*

God, today we celebrate life itself:
 In the mercy-full name of the Father,
 in the grace-full name of the Son,
 in the joy-full name of the Spirit,
we celebrate your incomparable gifts
 of life and love to us all!
O Friend of the earth,
 resource-full are you for ever!
Amen!

*Grant us the grace, O God,*
 *to know what is worth knowing,*
 *love what is worth loving,*
 *praise what pleases you most,*
 *value what is most precious to you,*
 *and to hate those things that offend you.*
*Give us discernment to judge*
 *between things that appear similar*
 *and to search out and do those things*
 *that delight and honour you.*
*Through Jesus Christ our Lord. Amen.*

*Thomas à Kempis, scholar, Germany, 1380-1471*

**September 30**

*Christ is the Alpha and the Omega; the beginning that cannot be expressed and the end that is beyond understanding.*
                                    *Melito, Bishop of Sardis, died c. 180*

Blessed are you, Saviour-Friend,
    the Joy of loving hearts!
You played our childhood,
    endured our adolescence,
shared our toil and sweat
    and our weary evenings.
You listened and cried,
    you laughed and sighed,
and having loved your own
    who are in this world
    you love us beyond the very end.
Hallelujah!

*Encouraged, O God, by the wealth of your love I will always celebrate life, even though I am lost for words or even for one adequate thought. Therefore, giving thanks in my mind, giving thanks in my heart, I exalt in you and I praise you, I adore you and I glorify you! You are the most holy God and Saviour, the most beautiful Spirit-Friend and Guide, my Brother, my Saviour and my Master. Amen and Amen!*
                        *Symeon, the New Theologian, Constantinople, 949-1022*

**October 1**

*No longer is there a single place or tiniest enclosure where the glory of Christ has not been poured out to the very ends of the earth and in highest heaven.*

*Melito, Bishop of Sardis, died c. 180*

I thank you, Holy Friend,
that one day I shall be wakened,
    not by light filtering through curtains
    nor by the singing of blackbird or kookaburra
    nor by the gentle kiss of a loved one,
but by the light of your eternal world
and the joy which nothing can destroy.
    Through your free and priceless grace,
    and to your eternal glory.
Amen!

*O Lord, support us all the day long of this troublesome life, until the shadows lengthen and the evening comes, the busy world is hushed, the fever of our life is over, and our work is done; then Lord, in your mercy, grant us a safe lodging, holy rest, and peace at the last; through Jesus Christ our Lord. Amen.*

*Anonymous, 19th century*

**October 2**

*We feel our crosses hard at times, but our courage should rise with them.*

> St. Mary MacKillop, social activist, Australia, 1842-1909

This day, O Wounded Healer,
    let your comfort and blessing be upon all
who wait with heavy hearts at hospitals,
    police stations, bus terminals and airports,
and with those who are waiting at home
    for a footstep which will never come.
In the name of Christ Jesus,
    who will never leave us comfortless.
Amen!

*Jesus, our Lord and Brother, you ask us to have our wits about us, that we are not led astray from you, nor panicked by shattering events. May we focus on you as the guarantor of the triumph of God over all that can harm or destroy us. Holy is your name forever. Amen.*

> Ron Gordon, UCA minister and writer, Australia, born 1932

**October 3**

*Words have always been the bane of religion as well as its vehicle.*
   *Walter Rauschenbusch, Baptist social activist, USA, 1861-1918*

Lord of the church, Lord of the city,
     may all Christians walk today
     in the shoes of the gospel of peace.
Empower them with the *shalom* of Jesus,
     so that in every street and school
     in every office, shop and market,
his good news may be seen and felt.
Amen!

*God bless this house*
     *from path to porch,*
     *from beam to wall,*
     *from door to window,*
     *from floor to ceiling,*
     *from room to room,*
     *from foundation to ridge cap:*
*God bless this house*
     *and all who call it home.*

                                        *Traditional Celtic blessing*

**October 4**

*The Trinity is like a mother's cloak in which the child finds a home
and lays its head on her breast.*
      *Mechthild of Magdeburg, mystic and social activist, Germany,*
                                           *c. 1207 – c. 1282*

With one soft Word
      you forged galaxies and poured light
      from numberless stars.
With one quiet Word
      you cradled planet earth
      and shaped its creatures.
With one loving Word
      you raised up humanity
      to be your family here.
And when we became set on self-destruction
      with one redeeming Word
      you defeated evil and death.
Awesome is your name, O God,
      and awesome are your saving ways,
Amen!

*Jesus, the salvation of those who sail on stormy seas, come, sail
along with me and soothe my voyage on this sea of life. And when
the sea of death roars in, sweeping all mortal comforts away,
whisper your word of Truth; "Peace! It is I." Amen!*
            *Attributed to Bishop Anatolius of Laodicea, philosopher,*
                                                    *3rd century*

**October 5**

*We did cultivate our land, but in a way different from the white man. We endeavoured to live with the land; they seem to live off it.*
        *Attributed to Tom Dystra, Indigenous Australian, 20th century*

Great Provider of every good and perfect gift,
    I marvel at how fertile mother earth can be,
    given the right conditions and the right care.
I pray for that new age when your people will trust
    the Fertile Spirit who alone can foster
    the greening of every mind and community,
and the fruiting of every human life,
    leading to a partnership with all creation
    and the surety that we are all God's family.
Amen!

*I vow and consecrate to God all that is in me:*
    *my memories and all my deeds to God the Father;*
    *my limited knowledge and all my words to the Son;*
    *my intentions and every thought to the Holy Spirit.*
*My heart, my tongue, my senses, and all my sorrows*
    *to the sacred Humanity of Jesus Christ,*
    *who was content to be betrayed into the hands*
    *of wicked men and suffer the torment of the Cross.*
        *Francis of Sales, priest and spiritual writer, Geneva, 1567-1622*

**October 6**

*These three things are of God; merciful words, true words, and the sweet singing words.*

*Traditional Irish saying*

This evening, God of numberless mercies,
    put your arms around your suffering ones
and gently cradle and comfort them
    through the long night hours.
Grant them the precious gift of deep sleep,
    that they may wake up tomorrow
stronger in body and mind
    better able to cope with whatever
pain and distress may be their lot.
    Through your Son Jesus,
whose hands never touched a person in vain;
Amen!

*Lord, Sweet Jesus, this life is full of trials and sufferings, and I have no other helper but you. Take me over then, Sweet Jesus, that I may be under your governance and your shepherding, and that my heart may never turn away from you, no matter how great the trial. But ever cleave to you, sweet Jesus. Amen.*

*Richard Rolle, mystic, England, c. 1300-1349*

**October 7**

*Love abounds in all things, excels from the depths to beyond the stars, is lovingly disposed to all things. Love is the kiss of God's peace.*
*Abbess Hildegard of Bingen, mystic-composer, Germany,*
*1098-1179*

God, when you command us to love you,
    with all that we have and are,
    you are not asking us to do you a favour.
You neither need our praise nor our flattery;
    no, you ask us to love you because
    only through such complete loving
can we reach our true human potential
    measured by nothing less
    that the full stature of Jesus Christ.
Thank you, holy Friend,
for that most blessed commandment.
Amen!

*Open our lives*
*to your lifted hands of blessing*
*release the songs of joy*
*birthed in this ruptured time*
*and let your house*
*be ours and mine.*
*Jennie Gordon, UCA minister and poet, Australia, born 1962*

**October 8**

*Love and compassion are necessities, not luxuries. For without them humanity cannot survive.*

*14th Dalai Lama, Tibet and India, born 1935*

God of today, yesterday, and tomorrow,
    we, the latecomers to this continent,
    pray for that glorious tomorrow
    when indigenous citizens will be honoured
    as our personal pastors and physicians,
    our teachers and trusted counselors,
    our good neighbours and prime ministers.
God, please help us to work to this end!
    Grant that this prayer may not remain
    just as a useless packet of pious words!
For Christ's sake;
    Amen!

*Lord of Light, may light defeat darkness in this land: may order triumph over chaos, peace over conflict, generosity over greed, honour over haughtiness; and may truth overcome the demons of deception here in this land.*

*The 'Jasna', Zoroastrian, c. 6th century BC*

**October 9**

*God has never left the world in complete and groping darkness; all religions contain some light from God. They are all from him.*
*Baron von Hügel, spiritual director, Austria and England,*
*1852-1925*

O my Christ Jesus!
    without you and your gift of faith,
my life would at its very best,
    be nothing but a dogged decency
carried on with many temptations
    among burgeoning technology
    and sustained by an angry defiance
    flung against the deep darkness
    of monstrous despair.
O my Christ Jesus, thank you for saving me
    from darkness and dread.
Amen!

*God, I thank you that you have not required us to fully comprehend Christianity; for if that were required, I would be of all men most miserable. The more I try to understand faith, the more it seems beyond understanding. I am most grateful that we only have to receive it and pray that, as we use it, our faith will increase more and more. Amen.*
*Soren Kierkegaard, philosopher, Denmark, 1813-1855*

**October 10**

*First bring justice to the orphan and protection to the widow, then
come and let us talk together, says the Lord.*
                    *Justin Martyr, early Christian apologist c. 100 – c. 165*

God of the eagle and the sparrow,
    of great leaders and common followers,
may your gospel swell in the hearts of all
    and your truth grow lovely in every mind.
May the mighty become meek
    and the meek gain strength,
may the foolish become wise
    and the clever learn simplicity.
O God, save our young nation
    and bless your inheritance.
In the name of Christ Jesus our Saviour.
    Amen!

*I praise you! You, O God, whose face is the object of the adoration
of all that yearn for you, whose presence is the hope of those who
are wholly devoted to your path, whose countenance is the
companion of those who have recognized your truth, whose name
is the inspiration of the souls that long to see your face, whose voice
is the true life of lovers, the words of whose mouth are the waters
of life to all in heaven and on earth!*
    *Adapted from Bahá'í Prayers, originally from Persia, 19th century*

**October 11**

*God is not only Fatherly, but is also a Mother who lifts her child on to her knee.*
> *Mechthild of Magdeburg, mystic and social activist, Germany,*
> *c. 1207 – c. 1282*

Wherever people suffer this day,
    dear motherly Spirit,
please support your loved ones
    on the pillows of your love.
Soothe away the stress and pain,
    ease all fear or angst,
and create a quiet pool of peace
    in every weary mind and soul.
In the name of Jesus,
    our scarred Healer and Lord.
Amen!

*Lord, teach me to seek you, for I cannot seek you unless you teach me, or ever find you unless you show yourself to me. Let me seek you in my desiring, and desire you in my seeking. Let me find you by loving you, and love you when I find you.*
> *St. Anselm, Archbishop of Canterbury, England, 1033-1109*

**October 12**

*Things eternal are more considerable than things temporal, and
things unseen are as certain as things that are seen.*
                                    *Wesleyan Covenant Service, England, 1883*


The gentle river, under low cloud,
    is like a polished slate
    reflecting reeds, ferns, trees;
a few gentle raindrops arrive
    creating magic circles;
    all is very quiet and filled
with a pure and elemental
    kind of knowledge,
    as if awash with eternity.
Thank you, for such 'time-out'
    when we can be still and know
    that you are indeed our God.
Amen!


*May none of God's wonderful works stay silent, by evening or
morning: shining stars, rugged mountains, rushing rivers, rolling
seas. May all things break into songs as we sing to Father, Son and
Holy Spirit. May all the angels in heaven respond: "Amen! Amen!
Amen! Power, praise, honour and glory to our God, the only Giver of
grace! Amen! Amen! Amen!"*
                                    *From Egyptian papyri , c. 300-400*

**October 13**

*Do not presume to speak to God as a wise man; come to him like a small child.*

*St. Isaac, Bishop of Syria, 7th century*

Lord Jesus, champion and saviour
    of the least and the last,
daily we witness the neglect
    of poorer and weaker citizens,
and hear of the frequent abuse
    of power, wealth and authority.
We pray for a government
    far better than we deserve,
and may all leaders embrace
    your saving grace and truth
which thrives in human weakness.
    For your love's sake.
Amen!

*My Lord and my God, take me from all*
    *that keeps me from you.*
*My Lord and my God,*
    *grant me all that leads me to You.*
*My Lord and my God,*
    *take me from myself*
    *and give me completely to you.*

*Nicholas of Flüe, hermit and mystic, Switzerland, 1417-1487*

**October 14**

*I do not find authentic godliness in the braying of a religious piety
but in deeds of love, undertaken without expecting any reward.*
                    *Magda Christopher, feminist author, Australia, born 1987*

God of Jesus, and our God,
save us from a religious hubris
    that boasts to have all the answers
    to all the big philosophical questions.
Bless us with a humble faith,
    ready to admit there is much
    we do not understand;
and give us the graciousness to
    live with such uncertainty
    throughout our whole life,
rather than fabricate and preach
    pretentious creeds
    or peddle pious clichés.
Amen!

*O God, sever me from self that I may be grateful to you. Let me
perish to self that I may be safe in you, and die to self, that I may
live in you. May I whither to self that I may blossom in you, be
emptied of self that I may become full of you and be nothing to
myself that I may be everything to you. Amen.*
                    *Desiderius Erasmus, scholar, Netherlands, 1466-1536*

**October 15**

*Better to be without logic than without feelings.*
                    *Charlotte Bronte, writer, England, 1816-1855*

God our Creator and Friend,
    we thank you for the desert lands
of the human spirit,
    where there is water to be found
in hidden springs or rock cisterns
    by those who are modest enough
to be taught by the old pilgrims
    and become humble enough to bend very low.
Amen!

*Untameable Spirit,*
    *teach me to fear you without being scared,*
*to love you without being pretentious,*
    *to serve you without being slavish,*
    *and to adore you without holding anything back.*
*Through Christ Jesus,*
    *my confidence and good health.*
*Amen!*
                    *Josh Doulos, pastor, Australia, born 1965*

**October 16**


*A master in the art of living simply pursues his vision of excellence through whatever he is doing, and leaves others to determine whether he is working or playing. To himself, he always appears to be doing both.*

> L.P. Jacks, Unitarian minister and philosopher, England,
> 1860-1955


For the skill of skaters and the craft of cooks,
    the strength of rowers and the muscles of miners,
for the rhythm of runners and the tenacity of teachers:
    the discipline of golfers and the delight of gardeners,
    for the surge of swimmers and the care of counsellors,
    the thrill of a goal and the patience of pastors,
we give all thanks and praise to you,
great Source, Soul and Sustenance of all
who live, move and celebrate their becoming.
Amen!


*We commend to your care, loving Lord, our souls and our bodies,*
*our feelings and our strengths, our desires and our goals.*
*We hand over to you, loving Lord, our prayers and our actions,*
*our work and relaxation, our health and our ailments.*
*We commend to you, loving Lord, our nearest and dearest,*
*our friends and benefactors, our neighbours and enemies.*

> *Adapted from Lancelot Andrewes, theologian, England, 1555-1626*

**October 17**

*God is not external to anyone, but is present with all things, though most men are ignorant that he is so.*
                    *Plotinus, Greek philosopher, Egypt, 204-170 BC*

God, even whenever we, the late-comers to these shores,
    pray for our indigenous sisters and brothers,
our understanding is flawed and even our best prayers
    remain tainted with some racism.
In your mercy, answer our prayers, not on our ignorant terms
    but in your most generous love and perfect understanding.
Through Christ our Saviour.
    Amen!

*God our Creator, I no longer strive to understand you or this puzzling world you have made. I cannot comprehend the reason for pain and suffering; I just want to relieve the distress of others. I pray that as I do it, I may discover a little more your nature: that you are the father of all people, and that the hairs of each head are numbered.*
                    *St. Francis of Assisi, friar, Italy, 1181-1226*

**October 18**

*why wait for death*
*to start to take apart*
*the closed and shuttered capsule*
*of your tightly guarded heart*
                    *Jennie Gordon, UCA minister and poet, Australia, born 1962*

Holy Friend,
when, unexpected as thieves, anxieties plunder us,
    gripping, bruising, mocking, confusing,
grant us the quick reflexes and the will
    to hold tight to your promises in Christ Jesus;
and those promises that we claim for ourselves,
    we pray may be granted to other people,
including our opponents and enemies;
    through Jesus Christ, our Saviour.
Amen!

*The music of our spinning world be yours,*
*music of magpie and rippling stream,*
*music of seas and wind in desert oaks:*
*the abiding music of the healing Redeemer*
*be always yours.*
                    *Adapted from a traditional Celtic payer*

**October 19**

*Remember we are but travellers here.*
                *St. Mary MacKillop, social activist, Australia, 1842-1909*

Blessed is your name,
    God of the universe,
    for the insistent questions
and the wild wonder
    that are awakened
when, far from city lights,
    we walk out at night
turn our eyes up to the heavens
    and take a long, long look
at the work of your fingers,
Amen!

*The One above me*
    *and the Three beneath me,*
*the One beside me here,*
    *the Three waiting for me yonder,*
*the One the ground under my feet,*
    *the Three the breath by which I live,*
*the One whose grace is beyond price;*
*the Three whose love is all in all.*
                        *Traditional Celtic affirmation*

**October 20**

*Is there even one atom in the universe that, in praise to God, does not dance with abandon?*
                              *Jalalaldin Rumi, poet-mystic, Afghanistan, 1207-1273*

Angry Christ
    challenging the ugly arrogance of power
    and cleansing the temple courts,
we who are rarely angry for the right reasons
    love, worship and adore you
    in the glory of your fiery love
    and the majesty of you sublime anger.
Awesome are you,
    truest, holiest Son of the earth!
Hallelujah!

*God of Joy, let us dislodge from our minds the notion that your joy can be a vacuous, religious thing, separated from deeds. Wherever the peasant tills the hard earth, there does your joy gush out in the greening of the corn; wherever a man displaces the tangled forest, and clears for his family a place for a home, there does your joy enfold them in peace.*
                              *Rabindranath Tagore, poet, India, 1861-1941*

**October 21**

*The smallest of human souls is still the daughter of the Father, the sister of the Son, the dearest friend of the Holy Spirit.*
*Mechthild of Magdeburg, mystic and social activist, Germany,*
*c. 1207 – c. 1282*

Holy Miracle of all things, seen and unseen,
please unveil enough of your holiness
    that we may be astounded with awe
    yet not paralysed by religious dread.
Should we ever falter in faith and slide toward the pit of fear,
send to us your Son Jesus, our true Brother,
    and speak through him your words of quietness:
    "Do not be afraid; it is really I."
Amen!

*Remove all fear from me, O Lord; graciously welcome me as I turn toward you. Cut off any of the bonds which restrict or afflict us, and keep us all under your sweet providence. May the stream of my life flow within the river of your righteousness. Do not allow my service to you end before its fulfilment, nor allow my song to be severed while I can still sing.*
*Attributed to the Rig-Veda, India, c. 1500 BC*

**October 22**

*The person whose love is the same for his enemies as for his friends,
is most dear to me.*
              *Bhagavad Gita, Hindu Scriptures, India, c. 600 BC*

Praise to you, Christ Jesus,
    for breaking down divisions
    and shaping a new community
    out of sinners and misfits.
Praise to you, Holy Spirit,
    for the new liberty
    and communal strength
    which enables us to reach out.
Praise to you, Fatherly God,
    for sustaining your church
    in spite of our foolishness
    and our abrasive ways.
Glorious is your daring!
    tireless is your caring!
Hallelujah!

*O blessed Jesus Christ, you invite all who carry heavy burdens to
come to you; please refresh us with your presence and power.
Quieten our understandings, and give ease to our hearts, by
bringing us close to things eternal.*
              *Evelyn Underhill, author and mystic, England, 1875-1941*

**October 23**

*For those who thirst in life's desert, there is a Well of sweetest water; yet it is only accessible to those who approach in silence.*
                              *From an Egyptian inscription, c. 1300 BC*

God, you are all-lovely and all-loving;
    my actual thirst for more of your Spirit
is in itself more satisfying than the gaining
    of all other goals or ideals.
So, I beg you, give me more of this sacred thirst
    and let all my days be filled
with this wonder-full, divine discontent,
    for herein lies the greater joy
and the only adoration which is eternally sustainable.
    Amen!

*Lift up our souls, O Lord, into the light of your presence; that there we may breathe freely, there repose in your love, there be at rest from ourselves, and from there return, arrayed in your peace, to do and bear what shall please you; for your holy name's sake. Amen.*
                *E.B. Pusey, theologian and scholar, England, 1800-1882*

**October 24**

*Like hairs on the head that are all numbered, we mere mortals are
joined to Jesus Christ, the head of all.*
                    *Abbess Hildegard of Bingen, mystic-composer, Germany,
                                                        1098-1179*

How ridiculous we are, God!
Bold with our science, surrounded with electronic gadgets,
    yet creatures of abysmal blindness
    when it comes to the loving things that ultimately matter.
Please send to our post-modern age that young Jewish healer
    who made a salve from common clay
    and touched the eyes of the blind.
May his touch enable us see ourselves as creatures
who are made truly made for worship,
    community, justice, mercy and peace.
Enable us to treasure our friends and pray for our enemies,
    to lovingly serve our neighbours
    and to seek first the realm of God.
Through Christ Jesus our Lord.
    Amen!

*Grant me, O God, prudence to avoid those who flatter me and
patience with those who contradict me, for it is a mark of grace to
be neither moved by flattery or angered by opposition; thus will I be
able to continue on securely in the course we have begun together.
Through Jesus Christ our Lord. Amen.*
        *Adapted from Thomas à Kempis, scholar, Germany, 1380-1471*

**October 25**

*As I wrestle with stories of his life, with the words Jesus said or which were attributed to him, with the mystery of his death and with the equally powerful mystery of the disciples' testimony to the resurrection, I cannot let him go – or perhaps I cannot be let go of, no matter how browned off I get with the church or aspects of it, no matter how distant I feel from the mystery of God, the man Jesus will not let me go.*

*Robert Renton, UCA minister and educationalist, Australia,*
*born 1946*

Grant to each of us, dear Jesus,
    both now and at the hour of my departing,
a committed soul that delights
    in this flawed yet beautiful world
    in which your Spirit is tirelessly at work.
yet which believes, trusts and strives
for that new world which is yet to fully come.
    Through you, our brother and guru,
the author and finisher of our faith.
Amen!

*Lord Jesus, as I kindle fire in my hearth this morning,*
*please kindle in my heart a flame of love;*
    *for my family, neighbours, strangers, friends and my foes:*
    *for the lowliest person who ever lived,*
*and to the Holy Three in highest heaven;*
*kindle a flame of love, a flame of love, O lord.*
*Amen!*

*Adapted from a traditional Celtic prayer*

**October 26**

*Children laugh as birds sing: because they are made that way.*
*Author unknown, USA, 20th century*

I rejoice, God and Father of all races and faces,
    for the infectious exuberance
    of Aboriginal children at play.
Please God, let not such energy and joy
    leach away into frustration and despair
    as they grow up and become adults.
Help us all in this weathered, old motherland
    to make sure there will be opportunities
    to develop and honour the gifts of each and all.
In Christ's name;
    Amen!

*You who are the life of all that draw breath, the help of those who come to you, the hope of those who cry to you, cleanse us from our sins, secret and open, eradicate any thought displeasing to you. Realign our souls, our hearts and consciences, so with a clean heart, clear soul, and Christ-like love, we may confidently and fearlessly pray – may your will be done on earth as in heaven!" Amen.*
*Coptic Liturgy of St. Basil, Egypt, c. 400*

**October 27**

*We are made for community. God is not a lone soloist, but is like one, holy trio of love, light and joy.*
                    *Magda Christopher, feminist author, Australia, born 1987*

Source of life and love, help us to see that cities
        are as much a part of nature as are termite mounds,
        rabbit warrens and hives of native bees.
Free us to exult in the good facets of city life
        as much as we applaud the virtues of rural living.
And give us both the will and wit
        to improve the quality of both city and country
as we fulfil your purposes for all peoples
        and to begin to truly glorify your name.
Amen!

*O Joy of all things, as we sense your playfulness, let our souls flame up to you like tongues of fire, flow with you like a great river, be permeated with your Being like the fragrance of flowers. For your name's sake. Amen.*
                                        *Author unknown, India*

**October 28**

*I may be silent but I am actually thinking; just because I do not chatter, don't treat me like a piece of wood.*

*Anonymous, Japan, 18th century*

God, our true Friend,
    unbind me from the delusion
    that what I think is of scant value,
but also from the desperate need
    to make myself seem important
    through overmuch prattle.
Free me from seeking significance
    from anything or anyone
    other than from your love for each and all.
Amen!

*Please grant me, loving Lord, to fulfil your high*
    *purposes in me, whatever they be.*
*Work in and through me, for I am born to serve you,*
    *to be your instrument, even if a blind one.*
*Therefore I do not ask to always see clearly,*
    *nor ask to know and understand it all.*
*I ask simply to be used when and how you will;*
    *that is sufficient for me.*
    *John Henry Newman, Cardinal, England and Ireland, 1801-1890*

**October 29**

*God, you come to me like dew on flowers, like the song of birds; yes and you give yourself, with all others, wholly to me.*
*Mechthild of Magdeburg, mystic and social activist, Germany,*
*c. 1207 – c. 1282*

Creator Spirit, thanks for the abundance of Creation:
    for bumble bee, brumby* and bison,
    for wallaby, whale and wildebeest,
    for reindeer, duckling and dairy herd.
Please help us to co-operate with you
    in cherishing all creatures great and small,
    not for what they can produce for us
    but for their very own sake
and to honour their Shaper and Sustainer.
Amen!

*\*brumby = Australian wild horse*

*Almighty God, whose glory the skies are telling, the earth your power and the seas your might, and whose greatness all feeling creatures herald; to you belongs all glory, honour, might, greatness and magnificence, now and for ever, to the ages of ages.*
*Amen!*

             *Liturgy of St. James, Antioch, early Christianity*

**October 30**

*How wonderful it is that nobody need wait a single moment before
starting to improve the world.*
                    *Attributed to Anne Frank, diarist, Netherlands, 1929-1945*

Wonderful God, some of us expect too much
    but many expect too little.
Muscle-in with your robust Spirit,
    that we may willingly attempt new patterns
    of thinking, serving and worshipping.
Toughen our faith to take big risks for you,
    and grant us the grace to launch into the deep
    and to make mistakes to your glory!
Give us the resilience to rise up from set-backs
    with an liberating Easter eagerness
    and a Pentecost impertinence!
From the rising of the sun to its going down,
    may your name be great among the nations!
Amen!

*Loving God, steady me when I stumble and pick me up should I fall.
Let this day add some knowledge or good beyond that of yesterday.
Oh, let me hear your loving-kindness in the morning, for in you I trust.*
                    *Lancelot Andrewes, theologian, England, 1555-1626*

**October 31**

*Look up, my people, the dawn is breaking*
*The world is waking to a bright new day;*
*When none defame us, no restriction tame us,*
*Nor colour shame us nor sneer dismay.*
*Oodgeroo Noonuccal, Indigenous poet, Australia, 1920-1993*

Quietly as the breath
    of the risen Christ infusing forgiveness
    as gift and mission on his disciples,
move, Spirit of mercy and light,
    on both old and new citizens of this land;
Let us fill our lungs with your best Gift
    from the living Lord Jesus,
that all may pray and serve tirelessly
    knowing that all things are being made new.
For the reconciliation of all races
    and to the eternal praise and glory of God;
Amen!

*With all my heart and soul, O God, I thank you, that in all the*
*changes and chances of this mortal life, I can look up to you, and*
*cheerfully resign my will to yours. I have trusted, you with my all;*
*my body and soul are in your hands. I do therefore know both*
*contentment and security, no matter what befalls me. Amen.*
*Thomas Wilson, Bishop, Isle of Man, 1663-1755*

**November 1   All Saints' Day**

*The One who governed the world before I was born shall certainly
take care of things once I am dead.*
>       *John Wesley, clergyman and evangelist, England, 1703-1791*

We thank you today,
Giver of time and eternity, for our fellowship
in the body of your church on earth and in heaven,
and for those Saints who in every generation,
have become like shining beacons of hope
in the shadow-lands of this ephemeral world.
We praise you for the Christlike way they lived
and for the fuller life they now enjoy with you
that inspires us to go and do likewise.
Amen!

*Dearest God, through your Sisterly Spirit you have made us
shareholders in the one, nurturing fellowship of the Saints. May we
continue to rejoice with the poor, stand with the meek, thirst with
the righteous, and be forgiving along with all your merciful children
on earth and in heaven. Then, at the last, gather us as one family
into the fullness of joy that you have prepared for us from the
foundation of all things. Through Jesus Christ. Amen*
>       *Magda Christopher, feminist author, Australia, born 1987*

## November 2  All Souls' Day

*The moon looks upon many night flowers; the night flowers see but one moon.*

*Jean Ingelow, poet, England, 1820-1897*

Eternal God, our ever-faithful Friend,
    now that our "dear and holy dead"
    are in another room of your house
where we can no longer see their smiles,
    nor hear the unique tones of each voice,
    nor reach out our arms to touch and hug them,
grant us enough love to truly let go of them for now,
    as they delight in the glorious company
    of those dear ones who have long preceded them.
God, let your perpetual light shine ever upon them,
    that their joy may be complete,
    forever and forever.
Amen!

*In the light of your peace, loving God, may even the valley of the shadow of death become as green pastures, and the vortex of death before us all as still waters. As we pass into that land which no mortal eyes have seen, may we be ready to greet those who have gone on ahead of us, and rejoice mightily that the days of sorrow and sin are no more.*

*James Martineau, Unitarian scholar, France, 1805-1900*

**November 3**

*A man's reach must exceed his grasp or what is a heaven for?*
                              *Robert Browning, poet, England, 1812-1889*

Saviour Jesus,
    if I become 'cheesed off' and cynical,
wake me up with some of your resurrection 'thing';
    if I settle for squalid attitudes and values,
stun me with a glimpse of your light;
    if I lapse into a trite and shallow faith,
pull the rug from under my feet;
    and if I act pious and arrogant,
trip me up before I can harm others;
    but should I stay faith-full and grace-full
then bless me with good cheer and serenity.
    For your name's sake;
Amen!

*Lift up our souls, O Lord, to the pure, serene light of your presence; that there we may breathe freely, there repose in your love, there may be at rest from ourselves; and from there return, arrayed in your peace, to do and bear what shall please you; for your holy name's sake. Amen.*
                              *E.B. Pusey, theologian and scholar, England, 1800-1882*

**November 4**

*The Holy Spirit is the harpist, and all human strings that are strung with love will make a sweet sound.*
    *Mechthild of Magdeburg, mystic and social activist, Germany,*
                                    *c. 1207 – c. 1282*

Forgive us, merciful God, for the discord and chaos
    that we, either perversely or in inadvertently,
    have set loose on the world around us.
Please help us to amend whatever we can,
    to retune ourselves to your Spirit,
 and to leave to your saving mercies
    the ultimate reconciliation of all things.
Through Jesus Christ:
Amen!

*Lord, sweet Jesus, this life is full of temptations and enemies, and help there is none save in you, dear Saviour. Take me then, sweet Jesus, to be under your rule and your shepherding so that your handiwork can never be undone. Take me wholly to your heart, that all my desiring may be for You who have wholly ransomed me, so that my heart may never turn towards temptation, but always cleave fast to you; for to love You, sweet Jesus is my most need, my most speed. Amen.*
    *Richard Rolle, mystic, England, c. 1300-1349*

**November 5**

*The Word of God has become human so that we might learn from him how a human being can become divine.*
*Clement of Alexandria, theologian, c. 150 – c. 215*

O wounded Healer,
    let your sensitive hands
rest on those sick and suffering people
    who are dear to their loved ones
and so utterly precious to you.

Let not agony overwhelm them by day,
    nor fears alarm them by night.
Asleep or awake, in hospital or at home,
    may these members of your family
find healing rest in your abiding care.
Amen!

*Almighty and everlasting God, who can banish all affliction both of soul and body; show forth the power of your aid upon those who are sick, that by the help of your mercy they may be restored to serve you afresh in holiness of living; though Jesus Christ our Lord. Amen.*
*Gelasian Prayers, France, c. 6th-7th century*

**November 6**

*Do all you can with the means at your disposal and calmly leave the rest to God.*
> *St. Mary MacKillop, social activist, Australia, 1842-1909*

Save us, dear Lord, from letting our love wear thin
    under the wear and tear of demanding neighbours.
Divert us from trying to do all that they ask,
    but also prevent us from closing the door
of compassion on those truly needy folk
    whom you do send our way for nurture.
Give to us a goodly measure of your discernment
    in saying yes or no to supplicants.
For your love's sake.
    Amen!

*Loving God, give us an open mind that we may know you, a willing attitude to serve you, and a passionate heart with which to love you. Go with us today in whatever we do, so that your light may shine through us. These things we eagerly pray, with your help may we fulfil them. Through Jesus Christ our Lord. Amen!*
> *Thomas More, scholar and statesman, England, 1478-1535*

**November 7**

*As you simplify your life-style, the laws of the universe will be simpler, solitude will not be loneliness, impoverishment will not be poverty, nor weakness a handicap.*
*Attributed to Henry David Thoreau, philosopher, USA, 1817-1862*

Lord of simplicity, we besotted technocrats
    are burdened and heavy-laden with possessions.
Our footprint on mother earth has become too heavy,
    and we fear for the well-being of the coming generations.
Please bless all those twenty-first century prophets
    who call us to radically repent and simplify our lifestyle.
    For the sake of all creatures great and small,
    both now, and throughout the ages that are to come.
Amen!

*Keep us from sin in all we do today, O Lord. Fill us with a holy simplicity, content to seek and do your will. Help us not to give short measure in return for the blessings you have given us. Preserve us in that true serenity that comes from unity with your will and purpose for all things. Amen*
*James Martineau, Unitarian scholar, France, 1805-1900*

**November 8**

*Divinity is in the enfolding and the unfolding of everything that is.*
 *Nicholas of Cusa, philosopher and theologian, Germany, 1401-1464*

Author of our days,
    each morning we give our hearts
    to you and you alone,
For there is nothing else
    worthy of your love
    that we can give;
nor is there any other gift
    that brings to our giving
    such delight and content.
Amen!

*We give thanks for our mother, the earth which sustains us.*
*We give thanks for the rivers, which supply us with water.*
*We give thanks for all herbs, which furnish medicines*
*that cure diseases.*
*We give thanks for the sun, that looks upon the earth*
*with a generous eye.*
*We give thanks for moon and stars, giving us their light*
*when the sun is gone.*
*Lastly, we give thanks to the Great Spirit, in whom is embodied*
*all goodness, who directs all things for the good of Her children.*
        *Attributed to an Iroquois Native American, USA, 19th century*

**November 9**

*I could tell you of heartbreak, hatred blind,*
*I could tell you of crimes that shame mankind,*
*But I'll tell instead of brave and fine*
*When lives of black and white entwine*
*And men in brotherhood combine.*
          *Oodgeroo Noonuccal, Indigenous poet, Australia, 1920-1993*


I thank and praise you, blessed Redeemer,
     for those choice First Australians
who with amazing grace are able to forgive
     our nation's crimes against them,
and so help full-fill your new creation
     where all things shall be reconciled;
where the lamb can dwell with the crocodile,
     the bilby lie down with the dingo,
     the baby play with a nest of young snakes;
where peace and justice shall encircle all people,
     and the earth shall be filled
     with the knowledge of God's love
     as the waters cover all the seabeds of the world.
Through Christ Jesus;
     Amen!


*O Lord, with a simplicity of heart, I offer myself to you today, to be*
*your servant forever; to obey you and to make my life a sacrifice of*
*praise. Amen.*
               *Thomas à Kempis, scholar, Germany, 1380-1471*

**November 10**

*Lord, show me not only what I can do today and but also what I should leave alone.*

*Elizabeth Fry, Quaker social reformer, 1780-1845*

Source of healing, God-with-us,
    as you were to a hemorrhaging woman,
    to a leper, and to the blind, deaf and dying,
    so be to all our suffering sisters and brothers.
As our hands reach out to the afflicted
    let them be as the hands of the Lord Jesus;
enlarge his ongoing ministry in us
    and bless every house of hope and healing.
For your love's sake;
Amen!

*To you, O Jesu, I direct my eyes;*
    *to you my hands, to you my bended knees;*
*To you my heart shall offer sacrifice;*
    *to you my thoughts, who my thoughts alone sees;*
*To you myself and all I give;*
    *to you I die and through you alone I'll live.*

*Attributed to Sir Walter Raleigh, writer and poet, England,*
*1552-1618*

**November 11**
*(See Appendix: Remembrance Day, Veterans Day, Armistice Day)*

*Even if I knew that tomorrow the world would go to pieces, I would still plant my apple tree. Everything that is done well in the world is done by hope.*
                    Martin Luther, protestant reformer, Germany, 1483-1546

Feet that climbed Galilean hills,
     ears that heard a Voice over the waters,
lips that spoke sentences of sanity,
     fingers that caressed a beggar's blindness,
body that felt a woman's touch of faith,
     mouth that drank the bitter cup of our futility,
smile that greeted friends on Easter morning:
     Daily you come among us as Saviour,
and at the end you will certainly come again
     full of your incomparable grace and truth.
Alleluia!

*Brother Jesus, Saviour and Master, I know that all have sinned as I have sinned, and each has added to the net of evil as I have done. Yet one better thing I also know that the magnitude of human stumbling can never extend beyond the measure of God's mercy.*
                              An early Christian Greek prayer

**November 12**

*If that thing which you wish to do won't burn, but if it will blacken, then leave it alone.*
*Susannah Wesley, scholar and educationalist, England, 1669-1742*


God of Jesus, save us from a pig-headedness
    that refuses ever to compromise;
save us also from making soft compromises
    when we should 'tough it out'.
By your Spirit of Truth,
    may we know one from the other.
Amen!


*Christ's life be in your speaking, his wisdom when you refrain.*
    *A smile like cherries on your cheeks until we meet again.*
*May the love that Jesus gives keep you from things profane.*
    *A smile like cherries on your cheeks until we meet again.*
*On highland passes, in forests deep, traversing glens, in grief or pain.*
    *A smile like cherries on your cheeks until we meet again.*
*The Blessed Jesus still uphold you, the Holy Spirit be your guide.*
    *The Shepherd Jesus still enfold you, The Holy Three at your side.*
                    *Adapted from a traditional Celtic blessing*

**November 13**

*Trust always in God – she will provide.*
          *Emmeline Pankhurst, political activist, England, 1858-1928*

Merciful God, Saviour of the lost, and the bewildered,
     you recognize and feel the distress of all those dear ones
     who are now so changed by Alzheimer's Disease.
With your ever-faithful, indwelling Spirit,
     deeper than anything we can copy or understand,
     continue to be their intimate loved one and enabler.
And God, please work on our own deep seated anxiety:
     remind us that if should we end up this way,
     you will still know us by name
     and number the hairs of our heads.
Through Jesus, the same yesterday, today and forever;
Amen!

*Father, I abandon myself into your hands; do with me what you will.*
*Whatever you may do I thank you: I am ready for all, I accept all.*
*Let only your will be done in me, and in all your creatures. I wish no*
*more than this, O Lord.*
          *Charles de Foucauld, monk-humanitarian, France, Nazareth and*
                                        *the Sahara, 1858-1916*

**November 14**

*I cannot teach you the prayer of the seas and the forests and the mountains . . . but if you listen in the stillness of the night you may hear them, speaking to you in . . . the rhythmic silence.*
> *Abbreviated from Kahlil Gibran, poet, Lebanon, 1883-1931*

O God, our event-full God
> the poverty of our human words
> frustrates our spoken worship.
We say we praise, extol and utterly adore you,
> yet we have not said a fraction of the wonder
> that throbs in our hearts.
Thank you for sending us composers and musicians
> who can convey our souls deeper than words
> and elevate our praise to another height.
Amen!

*Lord, make me to know you aright, that I may ever more love, enjoy and possess you. And since, in this life here below, I cannot attain this blessedness, let it at least grow in me day by day until I am fulfilled in the life that is to come. Amen.*
> *St. Anselm, Archbishop of Canterbury, England, 1033-1109*

**November 15**

*disciples under the influence of grace*
*wage love*
*that's universal.*
                    *Jennie Gordon, UCA minister and poet, Australia, born 1962*

Make our vision, loving God,
      as tall as Christ and as deep as his love.
Keep us amazed in a stable,
      adoring beneath a cross,
      and jubilant by an empty tomb.
With such a hope possessing us,
      let us serve you boldly,
      efficiently, lovingly and merrily.
For your Name's sake.
      Amen!

*With all my heart and soul, O God, I thank you that through the*
*changes and chances of this mortal life, I can let go of self and*
*cheerfully resign my spirit to you. I have no trust, O Father, in*
*myself; but I do believe you will preserve me from all evil; the wants*
*and wishes of my body are of much less value. I do therefore rest*
*my soul in your mercy with great security and satisfaction. Amen.*
                    *Thomas Wilson, Bishop, Isle of Man, 1663-1755*

**November 16**

*My new song must float like a feather on the breath of God.*
          *Abbess Hildegard of Bingen, mystic-composer, Germany,*
                              *1098-1179*

Spirit of renewal, quieten our worries
     and arouse our confidence,
that we may know it is not mere dream
     that you have welcomed us
     into your most blessed family.
Amen!

*Teach me quiet, as the grasses are still with new light,*
*teach me suffering, as old stones groan with memory,*
*teach me humility, as blossoms are humble with beginning,*
*teach me caring, as mothers nurture their young,*
*teach me courage, as the tree that stands alone,*
*teach me limitation, as the ant that crawls on the ground,*
*teach me freedom, as the eagle that soars in the sky,*
*teach me acceptance, as the leaves that die each fall,*
*teach me renewal, as the seed that rises in the spring,*
*teach me to forget myself, as melted snow forgets its life,*
*teach me kindness, as dry fields weep for joy with rain.*
                    *Attributed to a Native American, USA, date unknown*

**November 17**

*Bring me a worm than can comprehend man, and I will bring you a man who can comprehend God.*
        *John Wesley, clergyman and evangelist, England, 1703-1791*

Incognito Christ,
It's not hard to glimpse your presence
        in those who like us and affirm us;
but it's much harder to recognise you
        in people who deflate and irritate us,
Thank you, beloved Enemy of wilful blindness,
        for not letting us get away with such bias.
Please continue to confront and rebuke us
        and to speak your living Word to us
through folk who may seem to be abrasive critics.
        For our good health and to your glory;
Amen!

*Almighty God, the ultimate, sweet Mystery of life, you know our needs before we even ask, and our foolishness in what we ask for; we beg you to have compassion on our human ignorance, and those good things for which we are unworthy to ask, or because of our blindness we cannot know we lack, please dare to give us; through the trustworthiness of your Son, Jesus Christ our Lord. Amen.*
        *Adapted from Book of Common Prayer, England, 1549*

**November 18**

*Any attempt to explain why God is this being who acts in this way must finally give way to silence. This is not the silence of unbelief however. It is the silence of gratitude for God's possibility which begins where human possibility ends.*

*Norman Young, minister and theologian, Australia, born 1930*

God of the Living Lord Jesus,
    dare we come running like Peter and John,
from hiding among our many losses and defeats,
    to visit that one tomb which is absolutely empty?
Dare we look inside and truly believe
    in that vacancy which will rob us
of familiar old doubts and pessimisms
    which we have long harboured?
Dare we stake out life on this event
    and begin to live again with debonair faith
in this utterly new reality?
    Lord I believe, save me from my unbelief!
Amen!

*Loving God, you have chosen the weak things of the world to confound the mighty, please shed your light upon us who watch for you; that our lips may praise you, our meditations bless you, and our deeds glorify you.*

*Salisbury Prayers, England, c. 1100*

**November 19**

*One man's interest in a single bluebird is worth more than a complete but dry list of all the fauna and flora of a town.*
    *Attributed to Henry David Thoreau, philosopher, USA, 1817-1862*

Lord, bless and heal those ornery people
    who seem reluctant to openly show
    the compassionate side of their nature;
like this one elderly, bent-over man,
    his face worn into a perpetual scowl,
    who hobbles daily into the city square;
a cloud of pigeons flock to greet and surround him;
    with measured scorn he verbally abuses them,
    yet, opening a plastic bag, feeds them lavishly;
the bag empty, and with a last curse
    thrown over his over his shoulder,
    he hobbles back to the busy streets
    and disappears among the crowd.
Bless him, and all ornery souls like him,
    O Lord of all-sufficient love.
Amen!

*O Lord, my prayers seem dead, my feelings dead, and my heart is dead: but you are a living God and I cast myself upon you.*
    *William Bridge, minister and political writer, England, 1600-1670*

**November 20**

*I am the fiery life of Divine Wisdom, I ignite the beauty of the plains, I sparkle on the waters, I burn in the sun, and the moon, and the stars.*

*Abbess Hildegard of Bingen, mystic-composer, Germany, 1098-1179*

In our daily searching
    for nourishment of Spirit,
give us, dear Lord,
    the persistence of sea eagles
patrolling the ocean coasts
    willing to spend long hours
for the food they need
    to thrive in your creation.
For your name's sake.
Amen!

*God has said to me:*
    *'Dear Daughter, tread gently on the face of mother earth, for it is more fragile than you think. Deal kindly with the mighty oceans, for they are a womb of many mysteries. Look after the air above and around you for, should you harm it, there will be a curse on your children's children, even unto the fourth and fifth generation.'*
*Then I answered:*
    *'Here I am, dearest holy One. Come Lord Jesus come; come quickly, and tread this earth with me.'*

*Magda Christopher, feminist author, Australia, born 1987*

**November 21**

*Each day, as soon as the faithful awake and rise from bed, even before commencing any duty, they must first pray to God, and only then begin their work.*

> *Hippolytus, reformer and Bishop, Rome, c. 170 – c. 236*

Through you, living Lord Jesus,
we pledge ourselves to the faith
    that mercy is stronger than vengeance,
    hope is much stronger than cynicism,
    and peace shall have the final say
    over apathy and enmity.
Please assist us to make good this pledge
    in all the miscellaneous duties of life
    that from the from the rising of the sun
    until its going down great may be your name
    in our street, and among the nations.
Amen!

*I may travel alone, yet I'm never alone, for you, my God, are always with me. There is no need to be afraid when the Lord of both day and night is here beside me. Within your hand I am much safer than with an armed band.*

> *Attributed to St. Columba, missionary, Iona, 521-597*

**November 22**

*The Word of God has become human so that we might learn from him how a human being can become divine.*

*Clement of Alexandria, theologian, c. 150 – c. 215*

O wounded Healer,
    let your sensitive hands
rest on those suffering people
    who are so dear to their loved ones
and so very precious to you.
Let not agony overwhelm them by day,
    nor fears alarm them by night.
Asleep or awake, in hospital or at home,
    may these members of your family
 find healing rest in your abiding care.
Amen!

*Almighty and everlasting God, who can banish all affliction both of soul and body; show forth the power of your aid upon those who are sick, that by the help of your mercy they may be restored to serve you afresh in holiness of living; though Jesus Christ our Lord. Amen.*

*Gelasian Prayers, France, c. 6th-7th century*

**November 23**

*Come Lord Jesus, be our guest*
*and may our meal by you be blest.*
           Martin Luther, protestant reformer, Germany, 1483-1546

Lord,
sometimes the air
seems charged
with your Spirit's presence;
saturated and pulsing,
like a music
composed of pure love.

Then
is the panting soul
wondrously quietened,
for we can breathe well
on even a little
of this holy atmosphere.
Amen!

*How could I ever dare say "I am a needy person" when I possess so*
*great a treasure, or complain "I am thirsty" while having in*
*superabundance the living waters, or ask "who will give something*
*to me" though I already possess such abundance, or question*
*"where will I find God" when you are with me each moment of each*
*day.*
           Symeon, the New Theologian, Constantinople, 949-1022

**November 24**

*But human experience is usually paradoxical; that means incongruous with the phrases of current talk or even current philosophy.*
*Mary Anne Evans (pen name George Eliot) novelist and journalist,*
*England, 1819-1880*

There are days in this old world
    when I feel so at home
    that I wonder whether
    I might have sold my soul?
There are other days
    when I feel so alienated
    that I wonder whether
    I have become a crank?
Spirit of Pure truth,
    be my interpreter
    my discernment
    and my true belonging.
Amen!

*Most merciful God, the helper of all people, so strengthen us by your power that our sorrows may be turned into joy, and we may continually glorify your name; Though Jesus Christ our Lord. Amen.*
*Salisbury Prayers, England, c. 1100*

**November 25**


*May the Holy Spirit enkindle you with the fire of His Love so that you may persevere, unfailingly, in the love of His service.*

*Lady Julian of Norwich, mystic and theologian, England,*
*1342-1416*

When events
flow sluggishly
forcing me
to spend time
in muddy places,

Lord,
give me the grace
to make use
of mud
as successfully
as does
the mangrove tree.
Amen!


*The Father bless you in the glens,*
  *in valleys and corries,*
*the Son bless you on the slopes,*
  *on lochs and on seas,*
*the Spirit bless you on the passes,*
  *through storm and snow drift,*
*May the All-canny One bless you,*
  *Yes, bless you always.*

*Traditional Celtic blessing*

**November 26**


*Christ is the Alpha and the Omega; the Beginning that cannot be expressed and the End that is beyond understanding.*

                              *Melito, Bishop of Sardis, died c. 180*


Those caring eyes
    that noticed a sparrow fall,
accepting eyes
    that nurtured a fisherman's call,
weary eyes yet undeterred
    in a judgement hall,
glazed eyes in agony
    outside a city wall:
King Jesus, have mercy,
    now, upon us all.
Amen!


*Lord Jesus, though you were rich for our sake you became poor; give us grace, we humbly pray, to be ever ready and willing to serve, as you enable us, the needs of others, and to extend the blessing of your kingdom over all the world. Amen.*

                      *St. Augustine, Bishop of Hippo, North Africa, 354-430*

**November 27**


*The Galilean has been too great for our small hearts.*
*H.G. Wells, writer, England, 1866-1946*


Come, royal Jesus, come;
　　you who are you are the most
　　unlikely king this world has ever seen!
Your scandalous brand of royalty
　　turns life upside down,
granting the meek title to the earth,
　　giving sinners the keys of heaven;
Come among us again,
　　riding that ridiculous little donkey
and call us into that brave new world
　　where mercy is the only currency
and your grace is the pearl of great price.
　　Even so, Lord Jesus, come.
Amen!


*Almighty and ever-loving God, you have chosen to restore all things*
*in your well-beloved Son, our King and Lord. Mercifully grant that*
*all races and nations, may be brought under his most gentle and*
*loving yoke: who with you and the Holy, Spirit lives and reigns, ever*
*one God, world without end. Amen.*
*Salisbury Prayers, England, c. 1100*

**November 28**

*Blessed is the influence of one true, loving human soul on another.*
*Mary Anne Evans (pen name George Eliot) novelist and journalist,*
*England, 1819-1880*

King of a few barley loaves and fishes,
     within the peculiar arithmetic of your grace
     you can make much out of little.
Take over our small and cramped minds
     and the little parcel of our abilities,
     and give them your unique blessing,
so that within your commonwealth
     our gifts may multiply and expand
     in serving those for whom you died.
For your Name's sake;
Amen!

*Lord, you have set before us the great hope that your kingdom shall*
*come on earth; give us grace to discern its dawning, and to work for*
*that perfect day when your will shall be done on earth as it is in*
*heaven. Through Jesus Christ our Lord. Amen.*
  *Percy Dearmer, Canon of Westminster Abbey, England, 1867-1936*

**November 29**

*You have now become like the son of God. Yes, have become little Christs by receiving the Holy Spirit. You are now images of God once more.*

*Cyril, Bishop of Jerusalem, theologian, c. 313 – c. 386*

Lord Jesus,
    keep us alert to the needs
    and caring in our deeds,
of the sick,
the prisoner,
the hungry,
the friendless,
    that at your coming again
we may be ready,
Amen!

*Dearest Lord, may I see you today in the person of the sick, and while nursing them, minister unto you. Though you hide yourself behind the irritable, the demanding, and the unreasonable, may I still welcome you and say: "Jesus, my patient, how sweet it is to serve you." Amen.*

*Mother Teresa, religious sister and missionary, Calcutta, 1910-1997*

**November 30**


*To love someone means to see him as God intended him.*
                    *Fydor Dostoevsky, author, Russia, 1821-1881*



Galahs* are cheap, more plentiful than sparrows;
    they screech and scavenge across the countryside,
annoying blue wrens and infuriating farmers;
    galahs come in plagues; they seem dispensable.
Yet, on the highway there lies a dead one,
    broken awkwardly; a pathetic road-kill;
its life-long partner flutters near the corpse
    refusing to leave and join the flock,
    crying out in loyalty and grief.
O Great Friend of the earth,
    not one of your galahs is ever cheap!

*galah = a pink-grey parrot; also slang for a 'fool'.*



*Holy Threesome, Lord of night and day,*
*in my deeds and words, in wishes and my wants,*
    *in my meditating and thinking, in the meeting of my needs;*
*In my sleeping and dreaming, in my praying and hoping,*
    *in my body, mind and soul always;*
*May the Son of light and love,*
*the Son of delight and laughter,*
*the promised Child of Mary now dwell!*
    *Yes! Now dwell! Always.*
                                        *Traditional Celtic prayer*

**December 1**

*Remember to saddle your dreams before you ride them.*
                    *Mary Webb, author, England, 1881-1927*


That our Advent faith may ever be
    a creative, feisty enterprise,
and our loving of others
    a warmly held discipline,
come, Lord Jesus, come
    to the core of our being
and thoroughly possess our lives
    with your unmeasured joy;
in name of Emmanuel;
    Amen!


*You, eternal Christ, are all things to us. You are the Bridle of wild
donkeys, the supporting Wing of the eagle, the firm Tiller of ocean
ships, and Shepherd of the King's lambs. You are the delight of the
saints, the Word of the Most High, the Prince of wisdom, Workmate
of those who toil, Joy of the human family and the Song of God.*
                    *Clement of Alexandria, theologian, c. 150 – c. 215*

**December 2**

*It is not easy, speaking the truth in love. It is only by the grace of God that it can be done at all.*

*David Beswick, UCA minister and psychologist, Australia,*
*born 1933*

Holy God, we worship you;
    by your humble power,
    by your tireless travail,
    by your regenerating love
    and your saving grace,
we anticipate and embrace
    the reconciliation of all things,
and look to that final Day
    when nothing in the heavens
    or on earth will be left broken.
  Amen!

*Helper of all who turn to you, Light of those in the dark, Creator of all that grows from seed, Promoter of all spiritual growth, have mercy, loving Lord, on me and make me a temple fit for your residence.*

*From a 2nd century papyrus*

**December 3**


*I've never seen anyone rehabilitated by retributive punishment.*
                    *Henry Lawson, poet, Australia, 1867-1922*



God of all the prisoners who are 'on the inside',
      you know those who are justly incarcerated for crimes,
      and those who are the victims of miscarriage of justice;
Whatever the cause of their predicament,
      please bless each soul behind bars
      and nurture all ventures in rehabilitation.
As for those of us 'on the outside',
      confront us with the unpalatable truth
      that no one of us is free of wrongdoing.
Tell us again, lest we conveniently forget,
      that it is never your will or purpose
      that even one, poor soul should perish.
Through Christ our redeemer;
      Amen!



*I am bathing in Your blessing,*
*I am praying to be overflowed with*
      *the affection of God,*
      *the smile of God,*
      *the wisdom of God,*
      *the beauty of God,*
      *and the laughter of God,*
*as the saints and martyrs do*
*in the land of everlasting praises.*

                                    *Traditional Celtic prayer*

**December 4**

*Whatever weakens your reason, impairs the tenderness of your conscience, obscures your sense of God, or takes away your relish of spiritual things; that thing is sin to you, however innocent it may be in itself.*
  *Susannah Wesley, scholar and educationalist, England, 1669-1742*

Save us, loving God,
    from those odious comparisons
where we measure ourselves
    against other people.
Fix our eyes on nothing less
    than the full character of Jesus;
then, through repentance and re-creation,
    may we attain a little of his beauty.
For your love's sake;
Amen!

*Lord, grant that I may cease to crave the possessions of others. The ones I do have can be cumbersome, for wealth brings more pain than happiness, and those with riches become subservient to them. Henceforth, O God, give or take from me; I would rather be poor than drowned in things. Let me use what I do have for your service, and to be content. Amen.*
  *Adapted from a poem by Robert Herrick, cleric and poet, England,*
                                                        *1591-1674*

**December 5**

*One among you speaks your name*
*walks the road by which you came*
*knows the fear you try to hide*
*sees the light you lock inside.*
                    *Jennie Gordon, UCA minister and poet, Australia, born 1962*


Fountain of hope, Source of integrity,
    help us to recognise and disclaim
any pretence of having a superior faith
    or possessing a purer doctrine
    than do other persons or beliefs.
But also save us from that sick modesty
    which is reluctant to openly witness
to the wonder you have done for us
    in the advent of your true Son.
As we journey through this season,
    assist us to live with his infectious spirit,
fed by the sure hope that nothing
    on this earth or in heaven
can ever dim or negate the radiance
    of the Bethlehem happening.
Amen!


*Lord God, keep us so alert in the duties of our calling that we may*
*sleep in your peace and awake in your glory.*
                    *John Donne, poet and preacher, England, 1572-1631*

**December 6**

*Don't keep pulling yourself to pieces. Refuse to pander to a morbid interest in your own misdeeds. Learn to trust more. Be sorry, pick yourself up, shake yourself, and get on with things again.*
        *Evelyn Underhill, author and mystic, England, 1875-1941*

Enable each of us,
    God of the 'Aussie battlers,'
to reach high for the light
    as do soaring blue-gum trees.
Grant that in our reaching up
    towards the Advent light
we may also grow straight and tall
    with the integrity of Jesus.
Amen!

*O God, who has taught us that we are most truly free when we align our wills with yours, help us to gain this liberty by continual surrender to you, that we may walk in the way which you have ordained for us, and in doing your will we may find true life. Amen.*
        *Salisbury Prayers, England, c. 1100*

**December 7**

*I am always easy of belief when the creed pleases me.*
*Charlotte Bronte, writer, England, 1816-1855*

We, your children, O God,
    have become like magnets,
drawing to ourselves ideas
    that are superficially attractive.
Help us, God light, to seek those harder creeds
    which have no slick attraction,
and to entertain such awkward truths
    that can radically change lives,
turn old values on their head,
    break new ground in loving
and leave us gasping in surprise!
    Through Jesus Christ our Lord.
Amen!

*Lord Jesus, I long for more of your peace. If you give me your peace, there shall pour into my soul such a fullness of holy joy that this your poor servant shall be full of the melodies of praise.*
*Thomas à Kempis, scholar, Germany, 1380-1471*

**December 8**

*When I was young I was sure of everything. Now I am not half so sure of most things as I was before; at present, I am hardly sure of anything but what God has revealed to me.*
*John Wesley, clergyman and evangelist, England, 1703-1791*

Deliver us, Holy Friend God, from that arrogance
    which presumes to read the 'signs of the times'
and to make predictions that even your true Son
    would not deign to consider.
Keep us humble in believing and gentle in judging,
    wary in impulsiveness, calm in decision-making,
and faithful in serving the Master, Christ Jesus,
    the only author and finisher of our faith.
Amen!

*O Lord our God, make us watchful and keep us faithful, as we await the coming of your Son our Lord; that when he shall appear he shall not find us asleep on the job, but active in his service and joyful in his praise. For the glory of your holy name. Amen.*
*Gelasian Prayers, France, c. 6th-7th century*

**December 9**

*Religious emotion can become a substitute and counterfeit, and a*
*damage to the Reign of God among men.*
*Walter Rauschenbusch, Baptist social activist, USA, 1861-1918*

Loving God,
    in this busy lead up to Christmas
    we can become bone-weary.
In the hurly burly of challenging duties
    when my spirits may get flattened,
    firmly plant my footsteps in your ways.
    Even though my vision become distorted
    and my feet may want to drag,
    let me not fail to stay true with you.
Please grant me the grace-full resilience
    of a dogged yet optimistic faith.
Amen!

*Grant, O God, that in us the rough places will be made smooth, the*
*crooked straight, the mountains of pride brought low, and the*
*valleys of despondency lifted up. Prepare your way in us right now.*
*Blessed is he who comes in the name of the Lord. Amen!*
*Abbreviated from Samuel Osgood, artist, USA, 1808-1885*

**December 10**

*Repentance is an act of optimism and joy. It is turning away from something disastrous to something delightful; like turning back from stumbling around in a dark cavern to dancing through a field of sunlit flowers.*
                    *Magda Christopher, feminist author, Australia, born 1987*

As a child looks forward
    to its birthday party
    and a bride to her wedding,
 help us to look forward
    to that 'day of the Lord'
when we shall be complete
    even as you are complete,
God of grace and glory.
    Through the advent of Christ Jesus;
Amen!

*God, give to me once more the courage to hope. Merciful Lord, that I may practice hope, fructify my barren and infertile mind.*
                    *Soren Kierkegaard, philosopher, Denmark, 1813-1855*

**December 11**

*Life is but a bridge; travel over it but do not build your house upon it.*
*Attributed to Jesus, India, date unknown*

Mark this down, O my soul,
and keep it for me, O my Lord:
    the more of peace I feel
        by waterfall or seashore,
    the more captivated by the play
        of kangaroo or platypus,
    the more enraptured by the beauty
        of desert flowers or fiery sunrise,
    the more contentment I feel
        when enfolded by human love:
then the more convinced I am
that this world is not my true home.
    Amen!

*O Heavenly Father, thank you for taking care of me through the past night. Please show me similar kindness throughout this new day. When you call me from this earth, may I come home to you not as a creature of darkness but as a child of your Light. Through Jesus Christ our Lord. Amen.*

*Author unknown*

**December 12**

*A new attuning of all things has happened; as on a lyre one can play the same notes but change the rhythm, so is the Wisdom-Word changing everything.*

*Attributed to King Solomon, Jerusalem, c. 950 BC*

We rejoice with you, Lord of Advent,
    that our deliverance has already begun!
The eyes of the blind are being opened,
    and the ears of the deaf are unstopped.
The lame can leap like a kangaroo
    and the tongue of the dumb sings for joy.
The arid lands of the Outback rejoice
    and the deserts blossom as a rose garden,
The ransomed of the Lord return home
    with everlasting joy upon their heads.
Hallelujah!

*O God, you are the sun of righteousness and the light perpetual, giving gladness to all things; shine upon us both now and forever, that we may be glad and cheerful in you; Through Jesus Christ our Lord.*

*Early Christian, source unknown, c. 350*

**December 13**

*Beautiful music is the art of those prophets who can engage and calm the agitations of the soul; it is one of the most magnificent and delightful presents God has given us.*
> *Martin Luther, protestant reformer, Germany, 1483-1546*

Deliver us, God of awesome promises,
    from becoming sour Christians.
Let not fear, failure or misfortune,
    danger, disease or hardship,
grievous handicap or racking grief,
    turn us into dutiful yet dismal disciples.
Infuse us with merriment of your Spirit:
    good tidings to the meek and poor,
release of captives and sight for the blind,
    and garlands of praise instead of wreaths.
Through Jesus, "the Joy of hearts' desiring".
Amen!

*If I have faltered more or less in my great task of happiness; if I have moved among my race and showed no glorious morning face; Lord, your most pointed pleasure take and stab my spirit broad awake.*
> *R.L. Stevenson, novelist and poet, Scotland and Samoa, 1850-1894*

**December 14**

*Only a valid and compelling reason for loving this life passionately will cause us to advance further. Continue to regard us as an accidental offshoot or freak of nature and you will drive humankind into a state of revolt or disgust which will mean the definitive stoppage for civilisation on earth.*
        *Teilhard de Chardin, priest-scientist-mystic, France, 1881-1955*

We pray, Holy friend for all those dreary folk
    who have lost any reason to go on reaching for the stars:
intellectuals who have argued themselves out of optimism,
    common folk whose hopes has been sunk by misfortune.
May this Advent season penetrate their negativity
    and grant them enough light to restore their hope.
Through Jesus who comes among us
    with the *bonhomie* of hope and well-being.
Amen!

*Help me, O God, to put off all pretence and to find my true self; to discard all false pictures of you, whatever the cost to my comfort. Help us to let go of ourselves, so that we may give ourselves over to you, with all our strength, with all that we are and all we have.*
        *Jacob Boehme, shoemaker and mystic, Germany, 1575-1624*

**December 15**

*you can struggle to be free*
*but being caught is liberty.*
            Jennie Gordon, UCA minister and poet, Australia, born 1962

Most loving Creator, as the 'silly season' draws closer,
      we pray for the thousands of pet animals
      who may soon become unwanted Christmas presents.
Please God, stay the hand of any well-meaning giver
      who is likely to select such a gift impetuously,
and thoroughly discomfort the conscience of any recipient
      who, soon after the festivities are over,
      is tempted to mercilessly discard their pet.
In the name of the Holy One
who cherishes all creatures, great and small;
Amen!

*Be thou comforted, little dog, you too in the Resurrection shall have*
*a little golden tail.*
            Martin Luther, protestant reformer, Germany, 1483-1546

**December 16**


*When you were born, you cried and the world rejoiced. Live your life so that when you die, the world cries and you rejoice.*
*Attributed to White Elk, Native American, USA, date unknown*


Deep Source of my most sacred yearnings,
    I pray for the will and skill
to keenly enter into the profound territory
    of this fast-approaching festive season.
May I out-worship anything I've done
    through previous Christmas celebrations.
For Christ's sake;
    Amen!


*We give you thanks, O God, for the mighty yearning of the human heart for the coming of the Saviour. In our own souls we echo the sighs and aspirations of ancient men and women, and admit that our own souls are weak and in darkness without faith in him who comes to bring God to us and us to God. Amen.*
*Samuel Osgood, artist, USA, 1808-1885*

**December 17**

*[Each person can] find letters from God dropped in the street, and
every one is signed by God's name.*
                                    *Walt Whitman, poet, USA, 1819-1892*

Child of Mary, the 'dayspring from on high',
    you persist in bringing us out of darkness
    into the beauty of your glorious light.
Give us the pluck to walk in your light
    even though it shows up our shabbiness
and often makes us the laughing stock
    of those losers who sit in shadows and sneer.
Through Messiah Jesus, our Lord.
Amen!

*O young Shepherd, come again and seek me out, and lead me back
into your fold. Deal favourably with me in whatever way pleases
you, that I may remain in your keeping all the days of my life, and at
the end come to live at home with you, and with all those who are
already there, for ever and ever. Amen.*
                                    *St. Jerome, Bible translator, Bethlehem, 347-420*

**December 18**

*Young Mary had, as some might say in today's lingo, 'a bun in the oven'. Thank God she had! Without her travail, we would all be caught short with empty lunchboxes.*

*Josh Doulos, pastor, Australia, born 1965*

You restore us, O Lord God of hosts,
    you let your face shine that we might be saved.
You have stirred up your energy
    and have come among us with the gospel of peace.
Blessed are you, for choosing a young woman,
    the bearer of 'love divine all love excelling,
joy of heaven to earth come down';
    And we call his name Jesus, Saviour,
for he will indeed save his people from their sin.
    Hallelujah!

*Most Merciful God, helper of all people, so strengthen us by your enabling grace, that our losses may be turned into gains, and our sorrows into joyfulness; through Jesus Christ our Lord. Amen.*

*Salisbury Prayers, England, c. 1100*

**December 19**

*Let nothing disturb you. Let nothing frighten you. Everything passes away except God.*
  *Lady Julian of Norwich, mystic and theologian, England, 1342-1416*


O loving and most surprising God,
    grant to us the 'get-up-and-go' of Mary,
that we might be able to sincerely say
    in times of ease and days of travail:
"Here I am, Lord, I am your willing servant,
    let it happen to me according to your word."
Through Jesus Christ our Lord;
    Amen!


*Merciful and most loving God, who gave us your true Child who humbled himself that we might be exalted, and was incarnate in the Virgin Mary that he might uplift the down-trodden; please grant to us the inheritance of the meek and the vision of the pure in heart, and bring us at last to your everlasting beauty. Amen.*
                        *Prayers of Gaul, France, c. 6th-8th century*

**December 20**

*We have an agonizing need that only Christ can meet by coming right down into the dust with us.*
Evelyn Underhill, author and mystic, England, 1875-1941

You come, Lord Jesus, into the shadows
    of our trembling and questioning,
and like the purest white candle
    you give us sufficient light
in which to truly see each other
    as we rarely have before.
Please, Holy Friend, come to us now;
    don't allow us to squander
the opportunity of this holy season!
    Amen!

*All seeing God, grant that I, your fumbling servant, may hear as if for the first time the angelic song of the advent Gospel. Guide my feet to respond to its melody; and may the royal, immortal Christ who wards off evil from mere mortals, lead me to always fulfil your purpose for my being here. Amen.*
Adapted from Gregory of Nazianzus, theologian, c. 370

**December 21**

*Our real self lives in a place, as it were, between time and eternity, touching them both.*
                    *Meister Eckhart, author and mystic, Germany, 1260-1328*

The months of the years ebb away
    while we scurry around
    preoccupied with toxic worries,
rarely noticing the daily miracles
    of the One who is heaven-sent.
We thank you, God, for providing
    special times, like Advent,
when we can stop rushing
    and look deeply into another's eyes
at the heaven contained within.
    Hallelujah!

*O Christ my Lord, I pray that you will turn my heart to you from the depths of my being. With the noise of creatures around me silenced and the clamour of my own busy thoughts stilled, I shall spend time with you, where you are always present and where I love and worship you.*
                    *Leonard Lessius, theologian, Belgium, 1554-1623*

**December 22**

*no one has ever seen God*
*but*
*I have known heaven*
*in a Cup*
                *Jennie Gordon, UCA minister and poet, Australia, born 1962*


Here at this radio telescope I ponder
    how poorly, in spite of our astronomy,
    we really understand creation;
even a small child at Christmas may see
    more than some of the sharpest intellects
    observe via these mighty telescopes.
O Spirit of Truth, our intrepid Friend,
    please also reveal yourself to the clever
    and to the academic pundits,
so that your Logos may inspire and enrich
    all scientific endeavour.
May humility begin to reign on earth
    as it does in heaven.
Amen!


*O Almighty God, from whom every good prayer rises and who pours*
*out on all who sincerely want it, the spirit of grace and truth:*
*Deliver us from indifference of heart and arrogance of mind; that*
*with humble thoughts and kindled affections we may worship in*
*spirit and in truth; through Jesus Christ our Lord.*
  *Attributed to William Bright, church historian, England, 1824-1901*

**December 23**

*Blessed is the man or woman who comes as a little child to Christmas; such souls will experience the Wonder rather than theologise about it.*

*Magda Christopher, feminist author, Australia, born 1987*

When angels begin to sing their best
and shepherds listen in awe,
how much will prattling know-alls hear
upon the midnight clear?
Lord, have mercy,
Christ, have mercy,
Lord, have mercy.
Amen!

*Dear Lord Jesus, I want to thank you not just with my lips and heart, but also with my soul and deeds through which I can recognise and worship you. You are my all, and everything exists in and through you. By you I draw my daily breath, for you I awake and to you I sing. You are the only true Child of God, yet you have become my very own brother; to whom all honour and thanks are due, today, forever and forever. Amen.*

*Prayers of Gaul, France, c. 6th-8th century*

## December 24   Christmas Eve

*Did you now understand, my people, that Christ is the firstborn Child of God, begotten before the morning star?*

*Melito, Bishop of Sardis, died c. 180*

If familiarity has bred indifference, so that Christmas Eve no longer quickens the pulse;
    Lord have mercy.

If we are so busy putting the final touches to planned feasting and drinking that we have neglected our own spiritual preparation;
    Christ have mercy.

So that we may break out of the frenetic mood around us and make space in our hearts for the perpetual peace of Immanuel;
    Lord have mercy.

*O God, who has made this most sacred night to shine with the illumination of the True Light, grant, we beseech you, that as we have known the mystery of the Light upon earth, we may come finally to perfectly enjoy it in heaven; through the same Jesus Christ our Lord. Amen.*

*Gelasian Prayers, France, c. 6th-7th century*

**December 25   Christmas Day**


*there is a place*
*in each of us that waits*
*breathless and expectant*
*leading us*
*to that back room [stable] of our hearts*
*where Wonder lies wrapped*
*in flesh and cloth*
                *Jennie Gordon, UCA minister and poet, Australia, born 1962*



God of light and salvation,
    with orchestras and with massed choirs,
    with carols, gifts and feasting,
we celebrate the humble birth
    of your only True Child.
Open our minds to discern his truth
    and widen our hearts to receive his love,
that our lives may reverberate with your joy,
    and our deeds shine with your peace.
To your eternal glory;
    Hallelujah!



*Little Son of God, laid in a manger, we adore your coming! Now*
*God is of your body and ours! You are our Saviour and our brother*
*who sleeps in a crib, God is of our flesh and blood! Now there is no*
*difference at all between us. You lie in our misery, share our needs,*
*and assure us of glory. Halleluiah!*
                *Martin Luther, protestant reformer, Germany, 1483-1546*


*cont'd . . .*

**December 25   Christmas Day**  . . . *cont'd*

God Jesus, your Supreme Gift, we pray for those
    who are missing out this Christmas:
the cynic grown too hard to give gifts,
    the child born too poor to receive any,
and the rich who already have too much
    to appreciate any new present.
Through the mercy of your unspeakable Gift
    deliver your people from misery
    and its many causes and manifestations.
For Christ's sake. Amen!

*O God, help us to rightly remember the birth of Jesus, that we may share in the songs of angels, the gladness of shepherds. May Christmas morning make us happy to be your children, and Christmas evening bring us to our beds with grateful thoughts, as we forgive and are forgiven. For Jesus' sake. Amen.*
  *R.L. Stevenson, novelist and poet, Scotland and Samoa, 1850-1894*

**December 26**

*Our Lord Jesus knows the joy and pain of being human but sees beyond our limited range of vision to our real needs and destiny.*
                        *Ron Gordon, UCA minister and writer, Australia, born 1932*

Emmanuel,
    because of this holy Child,
Love Divine bends
    over every crib and cot
and every child is now
    eternally precious:
Thank you;
    Amen, and again we say Amen!

*God, who makes us glad with the yearly remembrance of the birth of your Son Jesus Christ: Grant that as we joyfully receive him as Redeemer so may we with sure confidence behold him when he shall come to be our Judge, who lives and reigns with you and the Holy Ghost, now and forever.*
                        *Book of Common Prayer, USA, 1928*

**December 27**

*Faith is a living, daring confidence in God's grace, so willing and certain that a man could stake his life on it a thousand times.*
        *Martin Luther, protestant reformer, Germany, 1483-1546*

As we grow older, Loving God,
        not much of the magic of Christmas remains;
yet how greatly does the Mystery deepen
        with the passage of each year!
Our juvenile ideas now seem trite,
        and even the dogmas of erudite minds
become ridiculously inadequate
        in the intimacy of this Emmanuel
who has chosen to be stabled among us
        with unspeakable grace-fullness!
Hallelujah!

*You, Holy Trinity, are a deep sea into which the more I immerse the more I find, and the more I find the more I want. My soul cannot be satiated in your abyss, for she continually hungers for you, yearning to find more of you in the light of your Light. As the deer thirsts for springs of water, so my soul thirsts to know you in deeper spirit and truth.*
        *St. Catherine of Siena, Dominican mystic, Italy, 1347-1380*

**December 28**

*God has become man so that man might become a god.*
                    St. Athanasius, Bishop of Alexandria, Egypt, c. 296-373

If I have been too much impressed by the impressive ,
     yet have been blind to the mini-miracles of our daily-ness;
if I have taken in by the trumpeting of our pop-culture,
     yet neglected the humble glory that is found in a baby's crib;
Lamb of God, have mercy up on me a sinner,
     stab me awake and convert me again
to the One who still comes to us in the weak, the poor,
     the sorrowing, the merciful, and the persecuted.
Amen!

*Merciful and most loving God, by your will and bounty Jesus Christ humbled himself, being born in a lowly stable that he might restore in me the celestial image, child of a young woman that I might become a child of God; grant unto me the blessed inheritance of the meek, that with all the saints I may glory in your perfect beauty. Through the same Jesus Christ our Lord.*
                    *Prayers of Gaul, France, c. 6th-8th century*

**December 29**


*While I drink my little glass of Wittenberg beer the gospel runs its course and overthrows empires.*
          *Martin Luther, protestant reformer, Germany, 1483-1546*


Most generous God,
     the enormity of your saving mercy is focused
     in the birth of Jesus, your only true Child.
Today we bring before you
     our largely unfocused lives,
our scatty thoughts and feelings
     and our unworthy words and deeds.
Please guide us to 'get things together':
     to praise you with all our heart,
to love you with a single mind,
     and to serve you with the zest
of the family of Christ Jesus;
Amen!


*God our Father, you have granted us in the advent of your holy Son, a fountain of life, bubbling up and making all things young again. In the fellowship of your Holy Spirit, may our regrets be transformed into hopes, our weakness into strength, our sins into mercy, and our distracted and fractured spirits into the mind of Christ Jesus; in his name by his grace. Amen.*
          *Author unknown, USA, maybe c. 1900*

**December 30**

*The past is only the present become invisible and mute; and because it is invisible and mute, its memorised glances and its murmurs are infinitely precious. We are tomorrow's past.*

*Mary Webb, author, England, 1881-1927*

God our holy Friend,
    you who never vary in your loving faithfulness
nor ever weary of making all things new,
    bless us as we near the end of this old year.
Do not permit our memories to be cruelled by guilt
    or governed by sentimental nostalgia.
Neither allow us to live in the museum of the past
    nor neglect its hard but enlightening lessons.
Don't allow us to reside in daydreams of the future
    nor neglect its exciting opportunities.
For your love's sake.
Amen!

*O Lord, my Maker and my Protector, you have graciously sent me into this world to work out my salvation; drive from me all those unquiet and perplexing thoughts that may mislead or hinder me in fulfilling those duties which you have asked of me. Grant this, O Lord, for Jesus Christ's sake, Amen.*

*Dr. Samuel Johnson, scholar, England, 1709-1784*

**December 31**

*The final thing, the Absolute in Christianity, is the experience not simply of contact with Christ, not simply a revelation given, not even of a deliverance wrought, but of a new creation in Christ. The Son is as creative as the Father.*
*P.T. Forsyth, theologian, England, 1848-1921*

I give you thanks, most faith-full God,
    for the year that is about to end
    with its fill of opportunities.
Although I have sometimes betrayed you,
    you have never let me down,
    not for one fraction of a second.
Your mercy has covered all my sins
    and has enhanced my better moments
    with your prodigal, loving-kindness.
Blessed are you, God of grace, mercy and truth,
    today, yesterday and forever!
Amen!

*O Lord, you alone know what is good for me; do therefore what you think best. Give to me or take from me, and grant that in loving confidence I may accept the orders of your providence and may equally adore all that comes to me from you. Amen.*
*Blaise Pascal, physicist and philosopher, France, 1623-1662*

# APPENDIX

## Prayers for Special Days

## Transfiguration

*God is the gladsome light of my very being.*
*Mechthild of Magdeburg, mystic and social activist, Germany,*
*c. 1207 – c. 1282*

Awesome Friend,
We glimpse your majesty in the night skies
    and your light in dew drops and children's eyes.
Yet much, much more we see your majesty
    in the transfiguring light of your love
both high on your mount of holy prayer
    down on the dusty plains of loving care;
then, at the climax, as your humble glory
    blazes through the darkness of the cross.
Confront us today with that Christ-Laser
    which brings disciples trembling to their knees,
 awakens unanswerable questions,
    and brings to birth our purest adoration.
For yours is 'True Light of True Light'
    for ever and ever!
Amen!

*We beg you, Lord Jesus, to graciously enlighten our hearts by your pure radiance; that we may serve you without fear all our lives. May we escape the darkness that can blanket us in this world, and one day, by your guidance, arrive at your land of eternal brightness. Amen.*

*Salisbury Prayers, England, c. 1100*

**Ash Wednesday**

*True repentance is a painful experience, analogous to being skinned alive.*

    *Attributed to D.R. Davies, preacher, England, 20th century*

Holy God, today we pause from the hectic,
    and often arrogant, projects of this world
(which are here today and gone tomorrow)
    to take our bearings and repent.
In your holy and all-knowing Presence
    we remember that we are all made dust
    and to dust we shall surely return
yet Christ shall give us life eternal!
    Amen!

                    .

*Blessed Redeemer, who for our sakes was content to bear sorrow and want and death: Grant to us such a measure of your Spirit that we may follow you in self-denial and tenderness of soul. Help us by your great love to succour the afflicted, to relieve the needy, the share the burdens of the heavy laden, and to ever recognise you in the poor and destitute; for your great mercy's sake. Amen.*

    *Brooke Foss Westcott, Bishop of Durham, England, 1825-1901*

## Palm/Passion Sunday

*I wonder if God sheds tears . . . and has been all these years?*
        *G.A. Studdert Kennedy, poet and priest, England, 1883-1929*

God of irrevocable love,
        as today we celebrate with the crowds
                who wave and shout "Hosanna",
please give us that feisty faith and hope
        which goes much deeper than religious hype
and engenders a love that is committed to go
                the whole way with Jesus
        to the Cross and beyond.
Amen!

*O God, who has chosen the weak things of the world to confound the mighty, please shed continual day upon us who watch for you; that our lips may bless you, our deeds may praise you, and our meditations glorify you. Amen.*
        *Salisbury Prayers, England, c. 1100*

**Maundy Thursday**

*As I think of Jesus with his friends at the Last Supper, I wonder: When he lifted up the cup, was it "to life", [l'kayim!] that he toasted?*

*B.D. Prewer, UCA minister, Australia, born 1931*

Sweet Jesus, lead us into that olive grove
    on the edge of town to pray awhile,
kneeling on a mat of little grey leaves
    while the paschal moon looks down.
Awaken us in your olive grove
    to the terrible mystery of saving grace
and the holy, bloodied sweat of purest love
    while the paschal moon looks down.
Steady us, Lord, in your olive grove
    that the tramp of arrogant feet
may not turn us into deserters,
    while the paschal moon looks down.
Amen!

*Lord Jesus Christ, for us your endured the horror of the deepening, darkest abyss; teach us by the depth of your anguish the vileness of all evil. So bind us to yourself in the fellowship of your sufferings that we may become united with you in your one, holy and sufficient sacrifice for all mankind. Amen.*

*Maybe - Frederick Temple, Archbishop of Canterbury, England*
*1821-1902*

**Good Friday**

*When Jesus came to Sydney they simply passed him by,*
*they wouldn't hurt a hair of him, just left him out to die.*
*The crowds went home and left the streets as empty as could be,*
*and Jesus crept against a wall and wept for Calvary.*
        *Adapted from G.A. Studdert Kennedy, poet and priest, England,*
                                                        *1883-1929*

God of the forsaken Jesus,
     here at your cross
we either abandon this world's wisdom
     and begin life again with you
or we must abandon you, God,
     and try to build some kind of existence
     on the bleak sands of despair.
Here at this Cross
     our faith either rises out of the darkness
     or falls into decay and bleak obsolescence.
Lord we believe,
     Save us from unbelief!
Amen!

*O Christ my Lord, who for my sin did hang upon the tree,*
*grant that your grace in me, poor wretch, may still engrafted be.*
*Grant that your pierced hands, which healed the sick and lame,*
*may move me to reach out my hand to serve and praise your name.*
        *Philip Howard, 20th Earl of Arundel, England, 1557-1595*

**Easter Day**

*The Resurrection? In my opinion the very future of Christianity is at stake on whether it confesses the risen Jesus half-heartedly and with a bad conscience or whether it does it joyfully and convincingly.*

*Gerhard Ebeling, theologian, Switzerland, 1912-2001*

May the surprise of Easter Day always confound your minds.
May the light of Easter dawn always shine in your eyes.
May the Easter laughter of the disciples be always in your ears.
May the rising path of the companion Christ be always under your feet.
May the footfall of the homely Christ be always at your door.
May the peace of the living Christ be always about your bed;
    Until that new day comes when your frayed mortality is no more,
    and the gift of abundant life and immortality with the Lord Jesus
    shall be your very own, intimate wonder and perpetual delight.
Amen!

*Easter Christ! You are the joy, the honour, the food and the delight of every creature. Through you the shadows of evil and death have fled, the gates of heaven are flung open, life is given to all. The human is now restored to the likeness of the Divine, and the lamps of our souls will never again burn out. Yours is the glory and the love forever and ever. Amen!*

*Hippolytus, reformer and bishop, Rome, c. 170 – c. 236*

*cont'd . . .*

**Easter Day**  . . . *cont'd*

Loving God, we thank and praise you
    for the wonder and mystery of Easter:
Baffling our human wisdom
    yet filling our minds with immortal truth,
bringing many unanswerable questions
    yet uplifting our faith,
challenging our religious assumptions,
    yet creating in us a cup overflowing with grace
to be eagerly shared with thirsty others
    irrespective of status, colour or race.
In the name of Christ Jesus;
Amen!

*You, who very early in the morning as the sun was just rising, merrily rose up from the dead, please raise us up daily into the newness of your own life, and save us; O Lord and Saviour, Jesus Christ. Amen.*

*Lancelot Andrewes, theologian, England, 1555-1626*

**Week of Prayer for Christian Unity**

*Christianity can only exist in the world as a Church [community] and not as a mere spiritual movement in the midst of society. We are members and shareholders of a great Spiritual corporation.*
                    *P.T. Forsyth, theologian, England, 1848-1921*

Gather us together, God;
    bring all into that one faith
    where old folk dream dreams
the young have new visions.
    and all things become possible.
Sweep us thoroughly with your wind,
    ignite our faith with tongues of your fire,
    set your love loose in our affairs,
until we begin to speak, sing and serve
    as those who are intoxicated with that Spirit
    who gets the morning stars singing together
and sets Christ's new world turning
    on the axis of amazing grace.
Bring us together, God,
    oh bring us together, now!
For Christ's sake.
    Amen!

*O, Lord God, the one God, make your people one. Whatever our differences, may we always realise that we are one in Christ Jesus. Let not Satan break the bond of unity between believers, but let it become increasingly strengthened in our own lives, and that of all people everywhere. For Christ's sake, Amen!*
                    *Author unknown*

## Pentecost

*Those thinkers are mistaken who imagine they can define man's nature simply by uncovering ever deeper the numerous roots of his being in the material world. Far from eliminating Spirit, they merely confirm how it mingles with, and acts on, the material world like a leaven.*

*Teilhard de Chardin, priest-scientist-mystic, France, 1881-1955*

Holy Spirit, joy Divine,
    sometimes you come as a fierce wind,
    sweeping away litter which clutters our lives;
Sometimes you are as a soft breeze,
    whispering away the worries
    furrowed on our faces;
Sometimes you are as a deep calm;
    stilling our hyper-active thoughts
    and bringing rest at twilight.
Always you are the Spirit of Truth,
    hearing our searching questions
    with a Love too holy for ordinary words.
Thank you, Sister Spirit,
    for being who you are for us.
    Amen!

*Almighty and everlasting God, in you nothing is obscure and nothing dark; send forth your light into our hearts that I may delight in the brightness of your Son and, walking in his ways may not fall into temptation; through Jesus your beloved Son.*

*Gregorian Prayers – a compilation, Rome, c. 600*

**Trinity Sunday**

*Tell me how it is that in this room there are three candles and but one light, and I will explain to you the mode of the divine existence.*
*John Wesley, clergyman and evangelist, England, 1703-1791*

Three Person'd God, you are the source and song
of all good gifts both seen and unseen,
    have pity on our search to comprehend you,
    forgive our itch to tame and 'creedify' you,
    and scatter the fences we may try to erect around you.
Let it be sufficient that you wonderfully bless us
    with your Parental providence,
    your Brotherly redemption,
    and your Sisterly regeneration.
In the name of the Father, and of the Son,
and of the Holy Spirit.
Amen!

*You, eternal Trinity, are a deep sea, into which the more I enter the more I find, and the more I find the more I seek. The soul cannot be satiated in your abyss, for she continually hungers after you, the eternal Trinity, desiring to see you with the light of light. As the tongue desires springs of running water, so my soul desires to leave this dark body to see you in truth. O abyss, O eternal Godhead, O sea profound, what more could you give me other than yourself? Amen!*
*St. Catherine of Siena, Dominican mystic, Italy, 1347-1380*

**Anzac Day in Australia and New Zealand**

*There is not room for death, nor atom that Christ would render void; you are Being and Breath, and what you are may never be destroyed.*

*Emily Bronte, poet, England, 1818- 1848*

God, our eternal dwelling place, comfort us as we bow before you on this sweet-sour day of remembrance. We think of the host of young men and women, who sacrificed their lives in the hope of peace on earth.

For the "dear and holy dead" who were husbands or wives, mothers, fathers, daughters, sons, sisters, brothers, cousins, grandparents, aunts, uncles, nieces or nephews.
*In light perpetual may they rest, and rise up, in peace.*

For the friends of childhood and youth who served side by side, for new friends made in training camps and for the mates that fell in the heat of battle.
*In light perpetual may they rest, and rise up, in peace.*

For all who enlisted eagerly, with the energy and hopes of youth; those who feared the cost, but nonetheless less went off to give of their best; those who, for ethical reasons, went reluctantly, yet under fire sacrificed their own lives for their mates.
*In light perpetual may they rest, and rise up, in peace.*

Also for our fallen enemies we pray: those who served dutifully and valiantly, and all who were forced to fight in conflicts they believed to be morally wrong.
*In light perpetual may they rest, and rise up, in peace.*

*cont'd . . .*

**Anzac Day in Australia and New Zealand**  . . . *cont'd*


God of the crucified Jesus, you alone fully understand the feelings of those still living among us who have returned home from war, leaving comrades lost at sea or buried in foreign soil.
*In light perpetual may they rest, and rise up, in peace.*

May we respect their painful memories, be inspired by their courage, and be ever ready to work beside all those who continue to keep the dream alive of peace on earth and good will among all people.
*For your love's sake.*
Amen!


*Almighty God, Father of all mercies and giver of all comfort, deal graciously we pray you with those who mourn, that casting every care on you, they may know the consolation of your love; through Jesus Christ our Lord. Amen.*

*Methodist Book of Offices, 1936*

## Thanksgiving Day, USA

*Do you want to know who you really are? Don't ask. Act! Your actions will delineate and define you.*
*Thomas Jefferson, third President of the USA, 1743-1826*


Give thanks to the Lord, all you people;
let all things praise the Lord for his goodness.

Give praise, earth, sky, and oceans,
    thank God from outer space.
Give praise you bold astronauts,
    thank God all children of the stars.
Give praise with all your light, sun and moon,
    thank God, you spiral galaxies.

Give praise from this beloved land, our home,
    thank God, you storms and fleecy clouds.
Give praise, lightning, hail, snow and ice,
    thank God, frost, rain, rushing streams.
Give praise mountains, plains and wooded hills,
    thank God, you cornfield, vineyard and cattle ranch.

Give praise bison, groundhog and puma,
    thank God, you eagle and hummingbird.
Give praise, grizzly bear and busy beaver,
    thank God, woodpecker and turkey.
Give praise, spawning salmon and singing whales,
    thank God, you squirrels and field mice.

*cont'd . . .*

**Thanksgiving Day, USA** . . . *cont'd*


Give praise, you Governors and President,
    thank God from Maine to Hawaii.
Give praise, you farmlands, towns and cities,
    thank God, you children and teenagers.
Give praise, scientist, pastor and parent,
    thank God from Alaska to Texas.

Give praise Native American and Pilgrim,
    thank God, you citizens of every race.
Lift up your cup of thanksgiving
    and call on the name of your Maker.
Let all things praise the Lord for his goodness,
    and his redeeming love for all people.
*Inspired by Psalm 148, Old Testament*



*O God, we thank you for this earth, our home; for the wide sky and blessed sun, for the salt sea and the running water, for everlasting hills and the never-resting winds, for trees and the common grass underfoot.*

*We thank you for our senses by which we hear the songs of birds, and see the splendour of the summer fields, and taste the autumn fruits, and rejoice in the feel of the snow, and smell the breath of spring.*

*Grant us a heart wide-open to all this beauty and save our souls from being so blind that we pass unseeing when even the common thornbush is aflame with your glory; O God, our Creator, who lives and reigns for ever.*
*Walter Rauschenbusch, Baptist social activist, USA, 1861-1918*

**Remembrance Day, Veterans Day & Armistice Day**

*Mankind is poised midway between the gods and the beasts.*
*Plotinus, Greek philosopher, Egypt, 204-170 BC*

God, our eternal dwelling place, comfort us as we bow before you on this sweet-sour day of remembrance.

We remember that mighty host of young men and women who sacrificed their lives, and those all who offered up their physical or mental health, in the hope of justice and peace on earth.

For those who are our sons or daughters husbands or wives, mothers, fathers; sisters, brothers, cousins, grandparents, uncles, aunts, nieces, nephews, neighbours or friends, we remember with solemn thanksgiving.

For all who enlisted eagerly, with the energy and hopes of youth; those who feared the cost, but nonetheless less went off to give of their best; and those who, for ethical reasons went reluctantly yet under fire sacrificed their own lives for their comrades.

For all those who are poignantly listed as 'missing in action', on land, sea and in air, for whom there is no known place of burial or memorial stone; and for those 'loners' who had neither family nor friend to mourn their loss.

For our fallen enemies, we also pray: those who served their nation dutifully and valiantly, and others who were compelled to fight in conflicts and battles they believed to be morally wrong, and for all their loved ones who continue to mourn their loss.

*cont'd . . .*

**Remembrance Day, Veterans Day & Armistice Day**

*. . . cont'd*

God of the crucified Jesus, you alone can fully understand and bless those veterans among us who have returned home from war, leaving behind the mortal remains of some of their comrades buried in foreign soil.

May we respect their painful memories, and work beside them as they labour to keep the dream alive of peace on earth and good will among men.

For your love's sake.

Amen!

*Unto You, O God, we look up for comfort, in you we confide our secrets, in your wisdom we trust, and on your love we repose; now and evermore. Amen.*

*Ancient Scottish Prayers*

# INDEX of THEMES

**Love/Loving:**

*Jan 1, 2, 3, 4, 5, 7, 8, 9, 11, 12, 13, 14, 16, 17, 20, 21, 26, 27, 28, 29, 31*

*Feb 1, 2, 3, 4, 5, 6, 7, 8, 11, 13, 14, 15, 16, 17, 18, 19, 20, 21, 22, 23, 24, 25, 26, 27, 29*

*Mar 1, 2, 3, 4, 5, 6, 7, 8, 9, 10, 12, 13, 14, 15, 17, 18, 19, 21, 23, 24, 25, 26, 27, 28, 29, 31*

*Apr 2, 3, 4, 5, 6, 7, 8, 9, 10, 11, 12, 14, 15, 17, 18, 20, 23, 27, 28, 29, 29*

*May 1, 2, 3, 4, 5, 7, 8, 9, 10, 11, 12, 13, 16, 17, 18, 19, 20, 21, 22, 23, 25, 26, 27, 28, 29, 30, 31*

*Jun 4, 5, 6, 8, 9, 10, 11, 15, 16, 17, 19, 23, 24, 25, 26, 27, 29, 30*

*Jul 1, 2, 3, 4, 5, 7, 8, 9, 12, 13, 14, 16, 17, 18, 19, 20, 21, 23, 24, 25, 26, 27, 28, 29, 31*

*Aug 1, 2, 3, 5, 6, 7, 8, 9, 10, 11, 13, 14, 15, 16, 18, 19,*

*20, 21, 22, 23, 25, 26, 27, 31*

*Sep 1, 2, 3, 5, 6, 7, 8, 10, 11, 12, 13, 14, 15, 16, 17, 18, 19, 21, 22, 23, 26, 29, 30*

*Oct 4, 7, 8, 10, 11, 13, 14, 15, 16, 17, 19, 20, 22, 23, 24, 25, 26, 27, 28, 30*

*Nov 2, 3, 4, 5, 6, 8, 9, 10, 12, 14, 15, 18, 19, 23, 25, 27, 28, 30*

*Dec 1, 2, 4, 7, 9, 11, 14, 15, 18, 19, 21, 25, 26, 27, 28, 29, 30, 31*

*Transfiguration*

*Ash Wednesday*

*Palm/Passion Sunday*

*Maundy Thursday*

*Easter Day*

*Week of Prayer*

*Pentecost*

*Anzac Day*

*Thanksgiving Day*

*Remembrance Day*

**M**

**Majesty:**

*May 10*

*Oct 20*

**Week of Prayer:**

*See Appendix*

**Wisdom:**

*Jan 2, 9, 22*

*Feb 3, 6, 10, 13, 14, 26*

*Apr 4, 18, 19, 28*

*May 3, 10, 21, 26*

*Jun 5, 6, 8, 10, 14, 21*

*Jul 4, 10, 11, 20, 26, 27*

*Aug 2, 16, 22*

*Sep 1, 9, 21, 28, 29*

*Nov 12, 20*

*Dec 1, 3, 12*

*Good Friday*

*Easter Day*

*Remembrance Day*

**Work:**

*Jan 3, 14, 28*

*Feb 4, 15, 18, 19, 21, 25*

*Mar 18*

*Apr 3, 22*

*May 2, 6, 9, 14, 18, 22, 29*

*Jun 2, 4, 19, 27, 30*

*Jul 1, 2 16*

*Aug 4, 24, 25, 29*

*Sep 2, 8, 22*

*Oct 1, 8, 16, 19, 25, 28*

*Nov 13, 21, 28*

*Dec 30*

*Anzac Day*

*Remembrance Day*

**Worry:**

*Jan 27*

*Mar 21, 28*

*Apr 7, 25*

*May 3*

*Jun 13*

*Jul 21*

*Aug 5*

*Nov 16*

*Dec 21*

*Pentecost*

**Z**

**Zealous:**

*Jan 4*

*Feb 11*

*Apr 10*

# INDEX of AUTHORS

On each day, the first prayer is an original by Bruce D. Prewer